D0724843

BASIC CATHOLIC BELIEFS
FOR TODAY

ACKNOWLEDGMENTS

I wish to thank two close friends, Mary Bryksinski and Norma McBride, who made invaluable suggestions and who patiently typed the first manuscript. A special appreciation to Father Jeffrey Mickler, S.S.P. for his theological insights, valuable notations and personal encouragement. I also extend my thanks to Brother Frank Sadowski, S.S.P., who edited the manuscript and made many contributions. I am also indebted to Margaret Counihan who typed the final manuscript. Particular thanks must go to Amy Bennett for her constructive suggestions, and exceptional insights.

Biblical quotations are from the Revised Standard Version.

Dedicated to my brother, Donatus, who is a loving brother, a considerate husband, a gentle father and a faithful son.

BASIC CATHOLIC BELIEFS FOR TODAY

FOR TODAY

The Creed Explained

by

Reverend Leonard F. Badia, Ph.D.

ALBA · HOUSE   NEW · YORK

SOCIETY OF ST. PAUL, 2187 VICTORY BLVD., STATEN ISLAND, NEW YORK 10314

Library of Congress Cataloging in Publication Data

Badia, Leonard F.
  Basic Catholic beliefs for today.

  Includes index.
  1. Catholic Church—Doctrines. I. Title.
BX1751.2.B223   1984   230'.2   84-14632
ISBN 0-8189-0469-0

Nihil Obstat:
Charles E. Diviney, P.A.
Censor

Imprimatur:
Otto L. Garcia
Chancellor
Diocese of Brooklyn
June 25, 1984

Designed, printed and bound in the United States of
America by the Fathers and Brothers of the
Society of St. Paul, 2187 Victory Boulevard,
Staten Island, New York 10314, as part of their
communications apostolate.

2 3 4 5 6 7 8 9 (Current Printing: first digit).

CONTENTS

ABBREVIATIONS

Old Testament

Genesis	Gn	Nehemiah	Ne	Baruch	Ba
Exodus	Ex	Tobit	Tb	Ezekiel	Ezk
Leviticus	Lv	Judith	Jdt	Daniel	Dn
Numbers	Nb	Esther	Est	Hosea	Ho
Deuteronomy	Dt	1 Maccabees	1 M	Joel	Jl
Joshua	Jos	2 Maccabees	2 M	Amos	Am
Judges	Jg	Job	Jb	Obadiah	Ob
Ruth	Rt	Psalms	Ps	Jonah	Jon
1 Samuel	1 S	Proverbs	Pr	Micah	Mi
2 Samuel	2 S	Ecclesiastes	Ec	Nahum	Na
1 Kings	1 K	Song of Songs	Sg	Habakkuk	Hab
2 Kings	2 K	Wisdom	Ws	Zephaniah	Zp
1 Chronicles	1 Ch	Sirach	Si	Haggai	Hg
2 Chronicles	2 Ch	Isaiah	Is	Malachi	Ml
Ezra	Ezr	Jeremiah	Jr	Zechariah	Zc
		Lamentations	Lm		

New Testament

Matthew	Mt	Ephesians	Ep	Hebrews	Heb
Mark	Mk	Philippians	Ph	James	Jm
Luke	Lk	Colossians	Col	1 Peter	1 P
John	Jn	1 Thessalonians	1 Th	2 Peter	2 P
Acts	Ac	2 Thessalonians	2 Th	1 John	1 Jn
Romans	Rm	1 Timothy	1 Tm	2 John	2 Jn
1 Corinthians	1 Cor	2 Timothy	2 Tm	3 John	3 Jn
2 Corinthians	2 Cor	Titus	Tt	Jude	Jude
Galatians	Gal	Philemon	Phm	Revelation	Rv

Introduction

A BRIEF HISTORY OF CATHOLIC DOGMA

In theological terminology, "dogma" can mean either a particular belief (for example, the Trinity) or it can be used to
describe a whole system of belief (for example, Christian dogma
as opposed to Jewish dogma). Prior to the eighteenth century,
the word was rarely used. The more common phrase was "article
of faith." For all practical purposes, the word "dogma" and the
phrase "article of faith" mean the same thing—that is, a teaching
which the official Church explicitly states as being revealed by
God. Dogmas are announced either by a General Council of the
Church or by a solemn official pronouncement by the Pope as
representative of the Church.

How did dogmas develop? After Jesus' Resurrection, His
followers preached His message. The infant Church (the community of Christians) grew in numbers. It became necessary to put
down in writing the life and teachings of Jesus. Thus came the
Gospels (50–100 A.D.). They contain the kernel of all dogmas
of the Church. During the first three centuries, the Church was
persecuted at times. Early Church writers like Ignatius of Antioch,
Justin Martyr and Irenaeus of Lyons seriously debated various
theological questions. They had to answer the heresies that were
arising. These three centuries saw no less than twenty-two
heresies. By the fourth century a General Council was called,
the First Council of Nicaea (325 A.D.), to state the faith of the
Church. In other words, what are its dogmas. There followed
other General Councils to combat attacks against the Faith. There
was the First General Council of Constantinople (381 A.D.) and

the General Council of Chalcedon (451 A.D.). To date twenty-one General Councils have been held in the twenty centuries of Christianity. The Nicene Creed (more correctly, the Nicaeo-Constantinopolitan Profession of Faith) which Catholics recite every Sunday, was formulated at the First General Council of Constantinople.

The twelfth and thirteenth centuries saw the rise of various religious orders like the Franciscans and the Dominicans who had their own unique theologies. Because of the Protestant Reformation of the sixteenth century, the Catholic Church had to clarify its dogmatic teachings. In the seventeenth and eighteenth centuries, Theology was sub-divided into its dogmatic, moral, pastoral and historical aspects. Each area became a specialization. Unfortunately, in the next centuries, each of these disciplines became isolated at times from the others. Today, the various branches of Theology are treated in relationship to each other. The biblical foundations of the theological disciplines are especially stressed.

Another question can be asked: Do the meanings of dogmas change through the years? To answer the question simply, we would say that words take on additional meanings because of linguistic development. New shades of meaning emerge. Therefore, periodically, the Church has to reformulate the expression of a dogma in the common language of the day. Yet, the idea remains constant.

For example, today the word "person" has taken on a fuller meaning than it did centuries ago. So, when we speak of the personhood of Jesus, it has a different shade of meaning than it did in the first centuries of Christianity. Conversely, to understand the classical creeds and dogmatic definitions of the Church, we must keep in mind the technical meanings of the words used in them. The intended meaning of such words as "person," "being," and "substance," for example, may differ from our everyday usage. Simply put, dogmas do not change; but sometimes the terminology does.

What happens to a person who refuses to accept a dogma of the Church? To deny or refuse to accept such a dogma is to put oneself outside the Catholic faith and community. Such a person is technically called a heretic. Dogmas are the "Constitution" of the Church. They are the revealed truths of God. The Church is the custodian of these truths. She must see to it that they are passed on without distortion or error.

In conclusion, we shall mention the General Councils and Papal pronouncements that dealt specifically with dogmatic matters. We will not mention those General Councils that reiterated what a previous General Council had said. Also, not every General Council touched on dogmatic problems. Some dealt with disciplinary and organizational Church matters.

First of all, a Council is a gathering of the bishops of the Church, called together by the Pope (in the ancient Church, and in the East, the Emperor summoned a Council), in order to discuss questions of faith, morals, church discipline or guidance.

There are several types of Councils: 1) A General Council or Ecumenical Council consists of all the bishops of the Church, from all over the world, who have been summoned by the Pope. Their decrees become the law when the Pope announces them. 2) A Provincial Council is one which consists of bishops of a certain area, such as the northeastern part of the United States. 3) A National Council is a gathering of the bishops of one country. 4) A Diocesan Council is composed of the bishops and clergy of a diocese.

The Roman Catholic Church has been in existence almost two thousand years. It was founded by Jesus Christ, who appointed Peter as its first leader (Pope). As the Church grew in the world, it encountered problems and it had to face them. From Peter to the present Pope, each has had the responsibility of Jesus' commission: "All power is given to me in heaven and in earth. Go, therefore, teach all nations, baptizing them in the name of the Father, and the Son, and the Holy Spirit, teaching them to observe all things whatsoever I have commanded you; and behold I am with you all days even to the consummation of the world." (Mt 28:18–20).

Although problems and doctrinal controversies existed from the start, it was not until the fourth century (325 A.D.) that the Church had its first General Council. Here and in the rest of the book, the date of each Council will be given in parentheses. All dates in this book are A.D. unless otherwise noted.

Fourth Century—The First Ecumenical Council: Nicaea (325) condemned the heresy of Arius, an Alexandrian priest, who denied the divinity of Jesus.

—The Second Ecumenical Council: Constantinople (381) condemned Macedonius, who denied the divinity of the Holy Spirit, and Apollinaris, a bishop who claimed that Jesus had a human body but no human mind.

Fifth Century—The Third Ecumenical Council: Ephesus (431) stated that Mary was the mother of the human and divine person of Jesus. It condemned Nestorius, who taught that Mary was only the mother of the human nature of Jesus.

—The Fourth Ecumenical Council: Chalcedon (451) emphasized that Jesus had a human and a divine nature.

Seventh Century—The Sixth Ecumenical Council: Constantinople III (680–681) condemned Monothelitism, the doctrine that Christ had only one will. Monothelitism was an attempt to unite the factions in the Eastern Church, especially the Monophysites who taught that Christ had only one nature.

Twelfth Century—The Tenth Ecumenical Council: Lateran (1139) ended the Western schism caused by the false Pope

Anacletus II. It condemned certain ideas, such as the belief that there are only two sacraments (Baptism and Eucharist), and also the rejection of the baptism of infants.

—*The Eleventh Ecumenical Council*: Lateran III (1179) rejected the idea that only the New Testament was inspired, and the Manichaean idea that there are two Gods, one good and one evil.

Thirteenth Century—The Twelfth Ecumenical Council: Lateran IV (1215) condemned the sect of the Cathari. It defined the doctrine of transubstantiation—that is, that consecrated bread and wine change into the Body and Blood of Christ even though their appearance remains the same.

Fifteenth Century—The Sixteenth Ecumenical Council: Constance (1414–1418) condemned the teachings of John Wyclif and John Hus, who taught that the Church is made up of those who are predestined to go to heaven.

Sixteenth Century—The Nineteenth Ecumenical Council: Trent (1545–1563) legislated a genuine reform in reaction to the Protestant Reformation. It condemned the teachings of Luther, Calvin, Zwingli, and other Reformers, but left open the possibility of dialogue with Protestants in the future on open issues. It restructured the Church. It gave official teachings about the Bible and Tradition, original sin and justification, the seven sacraments, and the sacrifice of the Mass.

Nineteenth Century—The Twentieth Ecumenical Council: Vatican I (1869–1870) defined the primacy of the Pope and the infallibility of the Pope in matters of faith and doctrine.

Twentieth Century—The Twenty-first Ecumenical Council: Vatican II (1962–1965) was a pastoral council which re-examined Church discipline, restored the vernacular language to the liturgy, revised the sacramental rites, stressed the importance of the laity, and opened dialogue with non-Catholics.

In addition to these General Council statements, there are two Papal statements which are considered dogmas of the Church. The dogma of the Immaculate Conception states that Mary, the Mother of Jesus, was free from original sin from the very moment of her conception. It was issued by Pope Pius IX in 1854. The dogma of the Assumption states that Mary was assumed body and soul into heaven. It was issued by Pope Pius XII in 1950.

Having discussed the background of Dogmatic Theology, let us now examine the contents of the Creed which contains the dogmas of the Church.

WE BELIEVE IN ONE GOD

Chapter One

WE BELIEVE IN ONE GOD

Throughout history the question of God has been pondered and discussed. God has many names and attributes. The Church maintains that the existence of God and His essence can be known through reason and revelation.

The classical Aristotelian, *rational* arguments for the existence of God are the proofs of motion, causality, contingency and order. The argument from motion is based on the observation that every moving object has been set into motion by other elements. Inanimate objects are moved by gravity and the forces of nature. Plants are stimulated to grow through the energy of the Sun and the minerals of the earth. Animals are given life and motion by other animals and need food to continue in motion. The classical philosopher is able to deduce from *reason* that ultimately the universe itself had to be put into motion by an unmoved mover, which we call God. To put it in a nutshell, some being had to get the cosmic ball rolling.

The proof from causality is similar. It is based on the observation that every effect must have a cause. *Everything* we observe has been brought into existence by other things. If we trace the chain of cause and effect back to its ultimate origin we would come to a first cause that is the explanation of all other effects. This ultimate cause the philosopher calls God.

The argument from contingency is based on the observation that everything in creation relies on other things for its existence. It is possible, however, to imagine that any individual object might not exist. An individual chair, house, plant, rock, animal, etc. can cease to exist. It is not necessary for the existence of the totality of reality. If only contingent objects existed, it is conceivable that given an infinite amount of time stretching into the past, that no object existed. If this were true, then nothing could not exist since nothing can spring from nothing. Therefore, the classical philosopher concluded that there must exist a being that is not contingent but absolutely necessary to sustain in existence all of the contingent beings we observe. This necessary being the philosopher calls God.

The final classical argument for God's existence rests on the observation that all things move in an orderly fashion and fulfill their proper ends. This order and purpose in the universe indicates that an intelligence lies behind creation. This intelligent being that orders all things the philosopher calls God. All of these arguments for God's existence are based on *observation* and *reason*.

The Role of Faith and Revelation

The believer uses his or her reason but relies primarily on faith and revelation to demonstrate God's existence and essence. God's existence is clearly and constantly proclaimed throughout the Bible (the Old and New Testaments). The biblical message affirms clearly that God exists and is the Creator and Lord of the universe. He is the One, Holy, All-Powerful, Unchangeable, Living, Triune, and Loving God. The Bible is the chief source of God's revelation. Contrary to what some people may believe, the Bible did not fall from the heavens completely written. It consists of a number of books written by many authors over a period of a thousand years. They recorded the many ways in which people experienced God.

The Official Teaching of the Church (Magisterium)

In the long history of the Roman Catholic Church, there have been several important statements concerning God's revelation through the Bible. The following are statements from various Church Councils.

> Anyone who does not accept the whole of the Church's tradition both written [Old and New Testament] and unwritten, let him be accursed. (Second Council of Nicaea, 787).

> One and the same God is author of the Old and New Covenants, that is of the Law, of the prophets, and of the Gospels; for, by inspiration, one and the same Holy Spirit spoke to the Saints of both Covenants. With all respect she [the Church] accepts their books ... [there follows the list of books comprising Holy Scripture]. (Council of Florence, 1442)

> [This Council] receives and venerates with the same piety and reverence all the books of both Old and New Testaments—for God is the author of both. . . . If anyone shall not accept all these books in their entirety, with all their parts, as they are read in the Catholic Church and are contained in the ancient Latin Vulgate edition as sacred and canonical, and if anyone shall knowingly and deliberately reject the aforementioned traditions, let him be accursed. (The Council of Trent, 1546).

> And these books of the Old and New Testament are to be received as sacred and canonical, in their integrity, with all their parts, as they are enumerated in the decree of the said Council [of Trent], and are contained in the ancient Latin edition of the Vulgate . . . (The First Vatican Council, 1870).

> Those divinely revealed realities which are contained and presented in sacred Scripture have been committed to writing under the inspiration of the Holy Spirit. Holy Mother Church relying on the belief of the apostles, holds that the books of both the Old and New Testament in their entirety, with all their parts, are sacred and canonical because, having been written under the inspiration of the Holy Spirit, they have God as their author and have been handed on as such to the Church herself. In composing the sacred books, God chose men and while employed by Him they made use of their powers and abilities, so that with Him acting in them and through them, they, as true authors, consigned to writing everything and only those things which He wanted. (The Second Vatican Council, 1964).

The Bible records the revealing relationship of God with humanity. Dogmatic theology reflects on the nature and meaning of this relationship which is ongoing and comprehensive.

In response to the changing needs of the people of God and under the inspiration of the same Spirit that inspired the biblical authors, the Church encapsules essential truths of God's self-revelation in official "dogmatic" statements. The Great Councils of the Church for twenty centuries have played an especially important role in settling dogmatic disputes. As we approach each topic, we will look first to the Scriptures and then to the Councils to grasp the teachings of the Church.

Biblical Revelation and our Understanding of God

The Hebrews came to believe that there is one God and only one God. With Abraham, God began to reveal Himself in a new and definite way (Gn 12:1). He became the God of Abraham, Isaac and Jacob (Ex 6:3). The oldest name used for God by the Hebrews was EL (Lord of Heaven). Later on, the name of God is EL SHADDAI (the Almighty God). During Moses' time, God is called YAHWEH (He who is). God liberated the Hebrews from the oppression of Egypt and freely entered into a covenant with His people (Ex 20:2). During the Prophetic period (9th–6th century B.C.) the idea became clearer. Amos saw Yahweh as the very Lord of History (Am 9:7). For Hosea, Yahweh was the faithful and loving spouse of His people, demanding exclusive love in return (Ho 2:4). Jeremiah emphasized Yahweh's righteous anger with His people, and instilled hope in them for the future because Yahweh was a merciful God (Jr 33:14f). While Moses taught that God was the unique Lord and Creator, the prophets insisted on His moral qualities, such as mercy, justice and righteousness. Having experienced the horror of the Babylonian Exile, the Hebrews returned to their homeland with a very special reverence for God. God in the Old Testament is clearly shown as the

Creator and absolute Lord of the universe. He is transcendent, merciful, loving, just, righteous and personal.

The Old Testament speaks of God's evolving revelation; the New Testament speaks of the full revelation of Jesus Christ. He is presented as the Son of God the Father. The heart of the New Testament revelation is the Resurrection of Jesus and the promise of our own resurrection. The Synoptic Gospels (Matthew, Mark and Luke) tell us that Jesus is the Son of God who sends the Spirit upon those who believe in Him (Mt 3:13–17; Mk 1:9–11; Lk 11:13, 24:29). In the power of the Spirit, Jesus inaugurates on earth the Kingdom of God. The Acts of the Apostles describes the ministry of the first followers of Jesus and the working of the Holy Spirit in them (Ac 1:8; 2:1–21). In the letters of Paul, the central theme is that Jesus is Lord. The Gospel of John explicitly states that Jesus is the self-manifestation of God. He is the Word of God (Jn 1:1–18). The recurrent theme of the New Testament is Jesus' unique relationship to the Father, and His promise to send the Paraclete, the Spirit who would lead His people into the fullness of Truth. Jesus' followers proclaimed Him as Messiah, Lord, Son of God. In the New Testament, the triune nature of God is revealed.

The Five Main Attributes of God

The first attribute: God is One. The Council of Nicaea (325) proclaimed, "We believe in one God, the Father Almighty, Creator of all things visible and invisible . . ."; the First Council of Constantinople (381), "We believe in one God, Father omnipotent, maker of heaven and earth . . ."; the Fourth Lateran Council (1215), ". . . there is one, true, living God . . .".

The unity of God is the basic doctrine of the Old and New Testaments. The first clear affirmation of this is made to Moses: "I, the Lord, am your God . . . you shall not have other gods besides me . . ." (Ex 20:2f). Again and again, the Hebrew people are reminded by their prophets that there is one God: "I am the first and I am the last; besides me there is no god" (Is 44:6); "The Lord is the true God" (Jr 10:10). In fact, every Jewish person recites the ancient prayer called the Shema: "Hear O Israel, the Lord our God is one Lord; you shall love the Lord your God with all your heart and with all your soul and with all your might" (Dt 6:4–5). Monotheism formed the central dogma of Judaism. It is a rejection of belief in many gods (polytheism); of one chief god with subordinates (henotheism); and of two equal gods (Manichaean dualism).

The New Testament adopts the monotheism of the Old Testament as an established truth. It affirms that the God of Jesus is the God of Moses and the Prophets. "They saw the dumb speaking, the maimed whole, the lame walking, and the blind seeing; and they glorified the God of Israel" (Mt 15:31). "Blessed be the Lord God of Israel for he has visited and redeemed his people" (Lk 1:68). "He who gives me glory is the Father, the very one you claim for your God" (Jn 8:54). "The God of Abraham and of Isaac and of Jacob, the God of our fathers, glorified his servant Jesus . . ." (Ac 3:13). "Or is God the God of the Jews only? Is he not the God of the Gentiles also?" (Rm 3:29). "But when the time had fully come, God sent forth his Son, born of woman, born under the law" (Gal 4:4). ". . . and there is no God but one" (1 Cor 8:4).

The New Testament clearly rejects all forms of polytheism, henotheism and dualism.

The second attribute: God is Holy. The Eleventh Council of Toledo (675), a small local Council, expressed the mind of the Church in its profession of faith when it said that the Trinity is "holy and ineffable." The holiness of God is often mentioned in the Old Testament. It was a favorite theme of Isaiah. At least 30 passages can be cited—for example, "They have forsaken the Lord, they have despised the Holy One of Israel" (Is 1:4). The prophet Hosea said, "I will not again destroy Ephraim, for I am God and not man, the Holy One in your midst and I will not come to destroy" (Ho 11:9). God's holiness demands that everything associated with Him be also holy—priests, Ark, Temple and people. The standards of ritual purity for the Hebrews are presented in Leviticus, chapters 17 to 26.

The New Testament rarely mentions the holiness of God. Yet many passages imply it. The sanctification of a person for a mission (cf Jr 1:5) is applied both to Jesus (Jn 10:36) and to the apostles (Jn 17:17, 19). However, the term "holiness" is more frequently applied to the Church and its members. Paul stresses this in his letters: The indwelling of the Spirit in the Christian makes him a holy temple (1 Cor 3:17); the Church as a whole is likewise a temple holy to the Lord (Ep 2:21). Holiness, therefore, is the essential condition for establishing contact with God, who is holiness Himself.

The third attribute: God is Just. The First Vatican Council (1870) referred to "God, Creator and Lord of heaven and earth, omnipotent, eternal, immense, incomprehensible, infinite in intellect and will, and in every way perfect" (Justice is therefore included). In the early Church, Irenaeus (2nd century) in his work *Against Heresies* (3:25:2–3), and Tertullian (3rd century) in his work *Against Marcion* (I–III), speak about the justice of God and that He is both just and punitive. The Hebrew word for "justice" includes the idea of righteousness. Yahweh's justice is therefore above all a loving care for the salvation of His people. Their well-being depends on His justice. In the Old Testament, the destruction of their enemies was taken as a sign that God's covenant (agreement) with His people was restored. Although sinners are punished, the justice of God invites them to penitence and promises redemption (Ezk 33:10–20). Justice is intimately connected with the covenant—that is, a person is righteous insofar as he or she is faithful to it.

In the Synoptic Gospels, the idea of justice appears more frequently in Matthew and Luke than it does in Mark. Justice often means condemnation; The Pharisees are threatened with condemnation (Mt 23:33; Mk 12:40). Paul threatens a number of people with judgment: slanderers (Rm 3:8), widows who break their pledge (1 Tm 5:12), heretics (Tt 3:11), evildoers (2 Th 2:12), and many others. In John's Gospel, Jesus is judge in the sense that He presents Himself as the object of decision. Those who do not believe in Him have already been judged.

Although righteousness for the Hebrew was attained by observance of the covenant with God, for the Christian this is accomplished through the death of Jesus Christ. The Christian must live in a way that is consistent with the death and Resurrection of Christ and with the new life of the Spirit.

The fourth attribute: God is Love. This is clearly stated in 1 Jn 3:11–24, 4:7–21. Two major Councils, the First Vatican Council (1870) and the Second Vatican Council (1962–1965) officially proclaim this.

The Old Testament speaks of God's love by using a special word, "loyalty." The images of a spouse and of a father exemplify this loyalty. The prophet Hosea (chap. 2) saw Israel as the spouse of Yahweh who was guilty of adultery when she violated the covenant. Jeremiah (2:1f) adopted this marriage imagery. He cites Israel's participation in the worship of the foreign god, Baal. Despite the Hebrews' infidelity he and the other prophets speak of God's love. For example, "I have loved you with an everlasting love; therefore, I have continued my faithfulness to you" (Jr 31:3). Parental imagery is expressed in many ways. The Israelites are called the children of the Lord (Dt 14:1). God's love is expressed in terms a father (Ho 11:1–4) or mother (Is 49:15f) would use.

In the Old Testament, Yahweh's love for non-Israelites is mentioned in connection with the establishment of His universal

kingdom (Is 2,2f; Mi 4:1–4; Jr 12:15). His love for the individual
is rarely mentioned (Ps 127:2; Is 48:14). Yet God's love for
certain kinds of people, e.g. the pure of heart (Pr 22:11) and the
virtuous (Pr 15:9), is more frequently mentioned.

In the New Testament, Jesus sums up the law of love by join-
ing two commandments: the love of God and the love of neighbor
(Mk 12:28–34). The Hebrews usually interpreted "neighbor" (cf
Lv 19:18) as meaning only a fellow Israelite. Hatred of Samaritans, for example, was permissible (cf Si 50:25–26; Jn 4:9).
Jesus, in line with the best prophetic tradition, universalized love.
God's love excludes no one (Mt 5:45); it cares for all the needs
of His children (Mt 6:25–32; Lk 12:22–31); it shows itself especially in His boundless mercy (Mt 18:12f; Lk 15).

Paul stresses that God showed His love by sending His Son
to die for sinners (Rm 5:8f; Tt 3:4). He makes no distinction
between God's love and Christ's love (Rm 8:37; 2 Th 2:16). God
pours His love into people by giving them His Holy Spirit (Rm
5:5). Paul speaks of God's love creating people anew (Gal 6:15;
2 Cor 5:17), making them His sons and heirs (Rm 8:14–17; Gal
4:4–7).

John's first epistle expresses it best: "God is love" (1 Jn
4:8). For John, the incarnate Son is the mediator of God's love
for men; He is the best proof of that love (Jn 3:16; 1 Jn 4:19).
John insists: "And this is His commandment, that we should
believe in the name of His Son Jesus Christ and love one another,
just as He has commanded us" (1 Jn 3:23).

In summary, the Old Testament commands the love of God
and neighbor. However, the New Testament adds a new insight
into God's love. God sends His Son, Jesus, to redeem all people.
And Jesus' command is to love all as God loves all. The Kingdom
Jesus proclaimed embraces people of every race and nationality.

The fifth attribute: God is Triune. Christians believe that in God
there are three Persons—the Father, the Son, and the Holy Spirit.

Each of these three Persons possesses one Divine Essence.

The Trinity's long doctrinal development can be traced as follows. a) The oldest doctrinal formulation of belief in the Trinity is reflected in the Apostles' Creed: "I believe in God the Father Almighty, maker of heaven and earth. And in Jesus Christ his only Son, our Lord, who was conceived by the Holy Spirit." This basic statement affirms the existence of three Persons but does not specify how they are interrelated and share in the same nature. b) The Council of Nicaea (325) stressed the true divinity of the Son and that He is of the same substance of the Father and is therefore an effective instrument of redemption. "We believe in one God, the Father almighty, creator of all things visible and invisible. And in one Lord Jesus Christ, the Son of God, only-begotten, born of the Father, that is, of the substance of the Father . . .". c) The First Council of Constantinople (381) stressed the equality of the divinity of the Holy Spirit with that of the Father and of the Son. "We believe in one God . . . and in the Holy Spirit, the Lord, the giver of life, who proceeds from the Father. Who together with the Father and the Son is worshipped and glorified." d) The Council of Chalcedon (451) firmly proclaimed the perfect union of divinity and humanity in Jesus and clearly declared the Nicaeo-Constantinopolitan Creed to be the belief of the Church. This is the Creed which Catholics recite each week at Mass.

The Roots of the Trinity

The Bible does not contain a clear, precise and technical statement on the Trinity such as is found in the Creeds. These statements may be considered as a kind of distillation and amplification of several statements in the New Testament about the Father, Son and Holy Spirit.

Traditionally, Christians have seen foreshadowings of this doctrine in the Old Testament. In this regard, it is important to avoid *eisegesis* (the reading into the Bible of something that is not there) and concentrate on *exegesis* (determining what the biblical authors actually meant).

We must always keep in mind that the Israelites approached God in a very concrete, non-abstract way. Rather than making clear and precise statements about Him, they described the Lord in imagery and word-pictures. Some writers tended to personify aspects of God (e.g., Wisdom, in Ecclesiastes and the Wisdom of Solomon). Some of the authors of the Bible, wanting to make sure that nothing would take away from the idea of God's absolute transcendence, attributed some of His acts to His Angel—understood in a way as being God's agent, manifesting the divine presence and serving as a bridge and buffer between the here-and-now and the absolute otherness of God. For example, Ex 3:2 calls the Being who appeared to Moses in the burning bush the "Angel of the Lord," but in Ex 3:4 He is "God Himself."

Other Old Testament verses refer to the Spirit of God, such as Is 11:2 and 32:15. Again, the idea is of something apart and yet not apart from the Lord, acting in our world.

There are other mysterious passages in the Old Testament which Christians have interpreted as hints of the Trinity. For example, in Gn 1:26 God speaks in the first person plural: "Let us make man in our image, after our likeness." In Is 9:6, the Messiah is referred to as "Mighty God." In Gn 18:2, three men appear to Abraham: one is the Lord, the other two are angels.

Some of the writers of the early Church, such as Eusebius of Caesarea, felt that the visible manifestations of God in the Old Testament should be attributed to the pre-incarnate Son. This idea did not find acceptance in the Church. It would be wrong to try to use these passages from the Old Testament as proof-texts to establish the doctrine of the Trinity. However, they do not contradict that doctrine, and Church writers from the very beginning (including the authors of the New Testament) have applied their imagery to the Members of the Trinity.

The word "Trinity" does not appear in the New Testament, but it contains the information on which that doctrine is based. Only a few decades after the Crucifixion, Paul writes in such a way as to imply that God and the Lord and the Spirit form a certain unity. This is illustrated in several passages: "The grace of the Lord Jesus Christ, and the love of God, and the fellowship of the Holy Spirit be with you all" (2 Cor 13:13). "I appeal to you, brethren, by our Lord Jesus Christ and by the love of the Spirit, to strive together with me in your prayers to God on my behalf" (Rm 15:30). "Blessed be the God and Father of our Lord Jesus Christ . . . in Him you also, who have heard the word of truth, the gospel of your salvation, and believed in Him, were sealed with the promised Holy Spirit . . ." (Ep 1:3,13). "Therefore I want you to understand that no one who speaks in the Spirit can say 'Jesus be cursed,' and no one can say 'Jesus is Lord,' except by the Holy Spirit" (1 Cor 12:3).

Since Paul treats all three, the Spirit, the Lord (Jesus), and God (the Father), as equal sources of divine gifts, their equal divine nature is implied. Their distinction is also indicated. These passages reflect beliefs prevalent among the early Christians years before Paul's letters were written.

A similar source for the dogma of the Trinity is found in Mt 28:19. "Go, therefore, and make disciples of all nations, baptizing them in the name of the Father, and of the Son, and of the Holy Spirit . . ." The Son and the Holy Spirit are placed on an equal par with the Father who is unquestionably God. Jesus' own baptism in the Synoptic accounts (Mt 3:16f; Mk 1:10f; Lk 3:21f) also has strong Trinitarian elements. The Gospel of John implies that the Father, Son and Holy Spirit are distinct persons (Jn 1:18, 33–34; 14:16,26; 15:26).

The Trinitarian Controversy

Throughout the centuries there have been many Trinitarian controversies. Errors in regard to the Trinity took the form of:

1) denying the real distinction of Persons (Monarchianism and Unitarianism); 2) denying the divinity of the Second or Third Person (Arianism, Macedonianism); or 3) denying the unity of the divine nature (John Philoponus, Roscelin of Compiegne, Joachim of Fiore and Anton Gunther).

The Monarchians (2nd century), Patripassionists and Sabellians were all Modalists. They held the belief that the Father, Son and Spirit were simply different modes, or expressions of one God. They were condemned by Pope Dionysius (259–268)

The Unitarians (16th century) deny the divinity of Christ and that there are three Persons in God. They were condemned by the Council of Trent (1545–1563). Like the Jews and Moslems, they stress the absolute transcendence and oneness of God.

The Arians were the strongest heretics with whom the early Church had to contend. They denied the divinity of Christ and taught that God the Son was not eternal. They held that Christ was a created being who partook of the divine nature as a reward for the work of redemption. This erroneous doctrine was condemned by the General Council of Nicaea (325).

The Macedonians denied the divinity of the Holy Spirit. The General Council of Constantinople (381) condemned them. Because there had been so much attention spent on the question of Christ's divinity, it took the Church longer to clearly define the divinity of the Holy Spirit.

John Philoponus (6th century) taught that the three divine Persons are three individuals of the God-Head just as Peter, James and John are individuals of the species of man. The Third Council of Constantinople (680) condemned him. His theory destroyed the essential unity of God. In a similar vein, Roscelin of Compiegne (11th century) taught that the three divine Persons are three separate realities. He was condemned at the Synod of Soissons (1093). Joachim of Fiore (13th century) also denied the unity of the divine nature because he thought of the oneness of the three Persons as a collective unity. The Fourth Lateran Council (1215) condemned his teaching.

Our developing understanding of the one true, triune God.

The Bible itself states that "no one has ever seen God" (Jn 1:18). And yet we talk about God. Where do we get our information about Him? How does He communicate to us? Does He communicate to some people more than others? Does He communicate directly or indirectly? How can I be sure that He has communicated to us? Where do I look for God's signals? These questions and others have eternally plagued humanity. The Christian also asks these questions and finds his or her answers in revelation.

In primitive religion, God or the gods are viewed as more powerful than human beings. This is indispensable for a sense of reverence. The Australian aborigines and the American Indians felt awe before the sacred. The forces of nature, such as fire and wind, were believed to be gods. The sacred mixed with the natural gives the primitive believer a sense of respect for the world. The ancient religions, like those of the Assyrians, Babylonians, Persians, Greeks and Romans, had a complex system of gods. For example, the Egyptians recognized Horus as the sun god, Osiris as the god of vegetation, and Anubis as the god of the dead. These religions were elaborate in belief and ritual. They transcended the simpler nature religions, yet by our standards they remained primitive.

Eventually, as human beings understood reality better, Polytheism gave way to Monotheism. Judaism contributed this notion to civilization roughly four thousand years ago. Most people are now able to see the superiority of belief in one God over belief in many gods. The Hebrews came to know the only living God by reflecting on His powerful intervention in their history. The Psalms expressed His mastery over life and death, His unfailing alertness and activity and His love for His people. In the book of Exodus, God shows His power over the Egyptians and their lifeless gods. The prophet Jeremiah stresses that God's power is unlimited—whether in Mesopotamia, Egypt, Canaan, Babylon or the heavens. No miracle is too great for Him. Finally, the Hebrews realized that He is a holy God. To them, holiness meant a separation from whatever is profane. Therefore, God demands that everything associated with Him be also holy: His priests, His temple and His people. Holiness therefore is an essential condition for establishing contact with God. God's holiness can then be communicated to the individual.

Christians believe that God's revelation to the Israelites reached its culmination in Jesus Christ. The New Testament expresses God's fullest revelation. It is Jesus who reveals the wider plan of God for humanity. The Synoptic Gospels show Jesus as the Son of God with authority. The Acts of the Apostles shows His disciples teaching and witnessing the gospel message. Paul the Apostle reminds his readers that Jesus is Lord and Savior of all. John's Gospel speaks of Jesus as the Word, the Son of God who reveals God the Father, and of the Paraclete who will deepen and protect this revelation in the hearts of believers.

Special Questions

Why doesn't God always answer our prayers the way we would like?

Recent surveys show that 94% of the American public believes in God. At times, it seems that God does not hear our prayers or hears but does not answer. This tests one's faith. It arouses real and urgent questions about the significance of prayer.

Alfred, Lord Tennyson wrote, "More things are wrought by prayer than this world dreams of." Yet people pray and their prayers sometimes seem to go unanswered. World or family or personal crises bring people to prayer. But prayer does not always resolve the crisis according to the individual's wishes.

Prayer is a dialogue with God. However, sometimes people bargain, threaten and make demands in this dialogue. They wheel and deal with God. What has happened in these situations is that people have forgotten the love of God. Love means that one cares for another. In this caring, one would not harm the other. God Who is love itself will not harm the person and will give to the individual all that is truly and ultimately beneficial. God cannot be forced to give what is harmful. He sees reality from a perspective superior to our own and one day we will appreciate why on occasion He has refused to respond positively to some of our more heartfelt prayers.

Then how should we pray? It must be with an openness to God's presence which makes us aware of His greatness and His sensitivity to us. Prayer attunes our mind to God's plan. We must pray with the realization that prayer does not effect a change in God, but in ourselves. To that extent, prayer affects historical events. A quick look at the past will illustrate this point. In the Old Testament, the disasters of the monarchy, the Babylonian Exile and other events show how the Hebrews did not have their minds in tune with God's plan for them. Instead we see how they tried to change His mind; they threatened God but instead suffered the consequences of their human stubbornness. The prophets warned their people to pray in the spirit of looking for the will of Yahweh who will save them. In the New Testament, the prayer of Jesus dominates the Gospels. Jesus teaches that the Christian must pray with complete assurance that his prayer will be answered in the best possible manner. In the Old and New Testaments, it is clear that the person praying must be aware of God's love and have trust in His direction. If this is done, we will never be disappointed in the results and fruits of prayer.

If God is good, why does He allow evil in the world?
This question is as difficult to answer as the question on prayer. There are no simple answers. Philosophically, three possible solutions have been offered. First, that God is not involved in our lives. He made the world and then left it to run itself.

Second, that God is directly involved in our lives: He causes evil. Third, that God does not cause evil, but allows it. This last point is at the heart of traditional Christian philosophy. However, none of the three solutions is completely satisfactory. Even the most pious believer, when personally touched by evil like Job, will cry out to God in anguish.

Evil—both moral and physical—exists in the world. Every day, our newspapers and our television screens tell us of it. Floods destroy numerous homes and towns. Children in the Third World die of starvation. Elderly people are mugged or killed in their homes and on city streets. Presidents and Popes alike are targets of assassins. Hundreds of refugees are slaughtered by invading forces. Young and old alike suffer from disease.

Evil is powerful. In the Bible, evil is personified by Satan, "the adversary." He incites David to make a census forbidded by Yahweh. He inflicts Job with disease. The Devil tempts Jesus in the wilderness (Mt 4:1; Mk 1:13; Lk 4:2). He enters into the heart of Judas. He goes about the world like a lion seeking to devour his prey (1 P 5:8).

Although we experience evil, we do experience good as well. Many "good samaritans"—family members, friends and strangers—exist. Many diseases are cured. People often forgive one another. Nature produces many beautiful sights for our eyes. We experience the laughter of children.

The struggle between good and evil continues. At times, it looks like evil will win out. Yet the world is still around despite the evil of men like Stalin, Hitler and others.

The problem of evil remains, but revelation in scripture and the tradition of the Church teaches that God will triumph. The love of God reveals itself in creation and salvation. His love is further revealed through His Son, Jesus, who communicates it to us. Jesus' message is that love will conquer, not evil. Our final thought on this problem comes from the theologian, Richard McBrien: "If it were not for our faith in the loving God, the existence of evil would not be so much of a problem. We might not even acknowledge evil as evil (and in fact, many who do not believe in God do evil and call it good)."

Discussion Questions

1. What arguments would you offer to someone who doesn't believe in God?
2. What does God mean?
3. What was the role of the prophets in the Old Testament?
4. Discuss the Book of Leviticus (ch. 17–26) on the notion of Holiness.
5. Why is John's Gospel so important in this problem of the One God?
6. What is a heretic? What do General Councils do for the Church?
7. Can you prove the existence of the Trinity from the New Testament?
8. Read and discuss Jn 1:29–35; 14:16–26.
9. Do you think the Arian heresy is still alive today? How?
10. Compare the statements quoted from the Council of Trent and the Second Vatican Council. Do you see any differences? If so, why?
11. Is the notion of God innate in human beings?
12. Explain how God's revelation continues today.

WE BELIEVE IN JESUS CHRIST

Chapter Two

WE BELIEVE IN JESUS CHRIST

Non-Christian Sources

Through the centuries, millions upon millions of people have been inspired by Jesus and His teachings. He has undeniably influenced the world more than any other single person. But what evidence do we have that He ever existed at all? Almost all of our information about Jesus comes from the four Gospels. The Roman writers Suetonius, Tacitus and Pliny the Younger, the Romano-Jewish historian Josephus, and the Jewish authors of the *Talmud* provide us with information about Jesus that confirms parts of the Gospels, and they also tell us something about the early Christian movement.

Some people have objected that these notices are too brief, and feel that the spectacular events of Jesus' life should have been famous all over the Roman Empire. Seen in the context of His times, however, it is clear that Jesus would not have attracted too much attention from the historians of Imperial Rome. Would-be Jewish messiahs were common in Palestine. There was usually one or more somewhere on the scene, trying to stir up a revolt against the Romans. Ac 21:38 mentions one of them. Crucifixion was an extremely common form of punishment, considered so degrading that it could not be inflicted on Roman citizens. When the apostles went out to spread the Gospel message, the casual observer would have been hard put to distinguish them from the legions of other itinerant preachers, such as the popular Cynic and Stoic orators. At first, it was almost impossible to distinguish between Jews and Christians. Within thirty years after the Crucifixion, however, the Roman authorities had made such a distinction.

In his *Lives of The Twelve Caesars*, written around 120 A.D., Suetonius provides a wealth of information about Roman politics in the days of Jesus and the apostles. In writing his book, he had access to secret government archives. In his life of the Emperor Claudius (A.D. 41–54), he writes: "Since the Jews constantly made disturbances at the instigation of Chrestus, he expelled them from Rome" (*Claudius*, 25). This took place in A.D. 49. In Corinth, Paul met the Jewish Christian couple Aquila and Priscilla, who were there because "an edict of Claudius had ordered all Jews to leave Rome" (Ac 18:2). As this shows that Christians were present in Rome at this early date, it would seem that the disturbances noted by Suetonius were religious quarrels between them and some other Jews. "Chrestus" was a common Roman mispronunciation of "Christus," and is mentioned by the early Christian writer Tertullian around 200 A.D.

In his life of Nero (A.D. 54–68), Suetonius writes: "Punishments were also inflicted on the Christians, a sect professing a new and mischievous religious belief" (*Nero*, 16). A clear distinction has by now been made between Jews and Christians.

Suetonius' contemporary, Tacitus, went into more detail in his *Annals*. In discussing the Christians put to death by Nero, he states: "They got their name from Christus, who was executed by sentence of the procurator Pontius Pilate in the reign of Tiberius. That checked the pernicious superstition for a short time, but it broke out afresh not only in Judaea, where the plague first arose, but in Rome itself, where all horrible and shameful things in the world collect and find a home" (*Annals*, IV:15:44). Like Suetonius, Tacitus based his work on Roman state records now no longer in existence. This quote shows that the Romans had detailed information on when and where Christianity was born, and that it was distinct from Judaism.

This is shown in another work by Tacitus, his *Histories*, in a fragment preserved by the Christian writer, Sulpicius Severus, in his *Chronicles* (*circa* A.D. 400). In his account of the Roman siege of Jerusalem in A.D. 70, Tacitus describes a debate in the Roman camp on whether the Temple should be destroyed. General (later Emperor) Titus and others held "the destruction of this temple to be a prime necessity in order to wipe out more completely the religion of the Jews and the Christians; for they urged that these religions, although hostile to each other, nevertheless sprang from the same sources; the Christians had grown out of the Jews: if the root were destroyed, the stock would easily perish" (*Chron*. 30).

Pliny the Younger, governor of Bithynia (in modern-day Turkey) and a contemporary of Tacitus and Suetonius, wrote to the Emperor Trajan around 111 A.D. about the Christians in his area. He mentioned that "on a settled day they assemble before dawn and sing a hymn of praise to Christ as a god."

The most detailed and controversial non-Christian account of Jesus comes from the Jewish historian, Flavius Josephus. Originally a participant in the Jewish revolt of A.D. 66–70, Josephus was captured by the Romans and predicted to Vespasian that he would become Emperor. When this took place, he was held in honor for the rest of his life by the Flavian dynasty (Vespasian, Titus and Domitian). This gave him the leisure to write his historical works, *The Jewish War* and *The Antiquities Of The Jews*. These works are of particular interest to the Christian because they describe people and groups mentioned in the Gospels and the Acts of the Apostles: John the Baptist, Pontius Pilate, Herod and his family, the Pharisees and Sadducees, Annas and Caiaphas, Felix and Festus.

In the *Antiquities*, Jesus is mentioned twice. In *Ant*. 20:200, mention is made of "the brother of Jesus, the so-called Christ, James by name." This would suggest that Jesus was described earlier, and we find him mentioned in *Ant*. 18:63. The almost universal consensus of scholars is that Josephus did write about Jesus here, but that his account was tampered with by Christian writers. In the early 1970's, an Arabic version of this passage was discovered, which is almost certainly close to what Josephus actually wrote.

Here is the tampered version, the traditional "Testimonium Flavianum" (Flavian Testimony):

> About this time arose Jesus, a wise man, if indeed it be lawful to call him a man. For he was a doer of wonderful deeds, and a teacher of men who gladly receive the truth. He drew to himself many both of the Jews and of the Gentiles. He was the Christ; and when Pilate, on the indictment of the principal men among us, had condemned him to the cross, those who had loved him at the first did not cease to do so, for he appeared to them again alive on the third day, the divine prophets having foretold these and ten thousand other wonderful things about him. And even to this day the race of Christians, who are named from him, has not died out.

Here is the more authentic version, preserved in Arabic:

> At this time there was a wise man who was called Jesus. And his conduct was good, and [he] was known to be virtuous. And many people from among the Jews and other nations became his disciples. Pilate condemned him to be crucified and to die. And those who had become his disciples did not abandon his discipleship. They reported that he had appeared to them three days after his crucifixion and that he was alive; accordingly, he was perhaps the messiah concerning whom the prophets have recounted wonders.

In his work *Against Celsus* (250 A.D.), the early Christian author and scholar, Origen, stated that Josephus did not believe in Jesus as the Messiah. In that same work, he cites another reference in the *Antiquities* to James the brother of Jesus. In it, the destruction of Jerusalem is attributed by some people to divine vengeance for James' death (both citations, *Against Celsus* 1:47).

Perhaps this passage was deleted by Christian copyists who felt that Jesus, not James, should have been named.

Another source of information on Jesus, independent from the Gospels, is found in the *Talmud*. Although this collection of rabbinic traditions was only put in its final form centuries after Christ, it contains material that is much older. Some of its brief references to Christianity reflect the tension that existed between Jews and Christians 50 or 60 years after the Crucifixion. Others seem to reflect hostile first-hand memories of Jesus. For instance, one passage reads in part: "On the eve of Passover they hanged Yeshu of Nazareth . . . he had practiced sorcery and beguiled and led astray Israel." In his *Dialogue with Trypho*, written around 155 A.D. but set twenty years earlier, Justin Martyr refers to similar charges: "they dared to call Him a magician who misled the people" (*Dial.* 69). The timing of Jesus' execution is independently confirmed by Jn 19:14. Similar charges against Him are mentioned in Lk 23:2, Mk 3:22 and Ac 6:14. Another Talmudic story mentions a saying of Jesus heard from one of His disciples, Jacob of Kefar Sekanya. Elsewhere, this same Jacob is described as offering to heal someone in Jesus' name.

These various non-Christian references to Jesus do not add much to what we learn about Jesus in the Gospels. They are valuable as independent witnesses of the fact that Jesus actually lived, and of the impact that the young Christian movement made on the world.

Christian Sources

If these references were all we had about Jesus, He would be a figure of no importance to us. He would merely be an obscure figure mentioned by a few ancient historians. Our truly important source of information about Jesus is divine revelation—embodied both in the Bible and in the tradition of the Church. From this source, we learn not only the historically verifiable aspects of

Jesus' life (such as the fact that He existed, performed wonders, had disciples and was crucified under Pilate) but also the things that transcend earthly history (that He is the Messiah and the second Person of the Trinity, the Son of God, that He rose from the dead, that the Church is His Body, that He is present in the Eucharist). The latter are matters of faith—they cannot be scientifically tested and proven.

Before considering what the Gospels tell us about Jesus, it is important to know what they *are* and *are not*. The Church teaches that the Gospels present a truthful picture of Jesus and His meaning for us. At the same time, it recognizes that they are complicated works which drew on a variety of written and oral sources available to the early Church. The Gospels concentrate more on the meaning of what Jesus did and taught, rather than on the exact details. Anyone reading the Gospels can see that there are innumerable differences in the details of their different versions of the same story.

The Gospels are not biographies, in the sense in which we normally use the word. They give us biographical information about Jesus, but they were not intended to give a complete account of His life. We have hardly anything about Jesus before His public ministry, while the events of the last few days of His life are told in great detail.

The reason for this is that the Gospels derive from the early Church's oral proclaiming of the Good News. As recorded in Ac 10:37–41 and 13:23–31, this proclamation mentioned Jesus' anointing by the Holy Spirit, the works of the Spirit in His public ministry, and His crucifixion, death and resurrection. The general outline would be the same, but the details would differ from preacher to preacher. At the same time, a great many stories and sayings of Jesus were remembered by the Church. Some of these seem to have been collected and written down before the Gospels were composed. These traditions varied according to the concerns of the local churches. Finally, when the inspired authors of our Gospels composed them (between 30 and 60 years after the

Crucifixion), the finished product reflected their own concerns and theological outlooks.

Some sayings and stories of Jesus were not included in the Gospels, but have come down to us either in the writings of the Church Fathers, or in additions or variant readings of some ancient Gospel manuscripts. One saying of Jesus not found in the Gospels is recorded in Ac 20:35.

What do the Gospels tell us about the life of Jesus? We can glean the following. Jesus was a descendant of King David. His mother was Mary, the wife of Joseph. He was born, according to Mt 2:1 and Lk 1:5, before the death of King Herod in 4 B.C. (the monk who, centuries later, divided dates into B.C./A.D. miscalculated by a few years). His family lived in Nazareth, a town in Galilee. He and Joseph were carpenters (Mk 6:3, Mt 13:55), skilled craftsmen who built houses and made ploughs, yokes and cabinets. Jesus was about 30 years old (Lk 3:23) when He began His public ministry, probably in 27 A.D. shortly after John the Baptist came on the scene (Lk 3:1). The length of Jesus' ministry is disputed. The Synoptics give the impression that it only lasted a year, but the Gospel of John indicates that it lasted at least three years. The latter view is probably more accurate. Jesus was already active in 28 A.D., 46 years after work on the Temple had begun (Jn 2:20). He was crucified under Pontius Pilate, the Procurator of Judea, either in 30 or 33 A.D.

Jesus' personality comes through vividly in the Gospels: passionate, zealous, merciful, stern, enigmatic. The heart of His message was that the Reign of God was at hand. He preached this in both Galilee and Judea, and worked wonders as a sign of God's presence. He had many followers, both men and women, but only twelve close disciples. He was misunderstood by many people, and His challenge to the religious establishment brought about His death. For the rest, the historian can only say with Josephus that Jesus' disciples "reported that he had appeared to them three days after his crucifixion and that he was alive."

The New Testament contains many "portraits" of Jesus. Each

inspired writer shows us a different facet of His life and mission. No single approach is definitive. Jesus is an inexhaustible subject.

The Testimony of the Synoptic Gospels

Matthew, Mark and Luke are called the Synoptic Gospels because they present Jesus from the same general point of view ("syn-opsis" means "same-eye"). Most of Mark's material is found in Matthew and Luke, and these latter two also share much of the same material. All biblical scholars acknowledge that these Gospels are closely related, but it is debated what exactly that relationship is. It is probably safe to say that Mark was written first, around 65 or 70 A.D., and that Matthew and Luke, both written about 20 years later, used it independently of each other. They also both used a collection of Jesus' sayings referred to by scholars as "Q." Matthew and Luke also each used other sources, either oral or written.

Mark may have been written to encourage the Christians who were persecuted under the Emperor Nero. The Jesus presented in this Gospel is a dynamic figure, always on the move, always performing great signs. Very few of His sayings are given. The Jesus of Mark is also an earthy figure, who gets angry, gets exasperated, and expresses amazement. The author of Mark often stops to explain Jewish customs to his readers—an indication that he was writing for Gentiles living outside of Palestine.

Matthew stresses the Jewishness of Jesus, and presents Him as the new Moses, the completer of the Law of Israel. This Gospel emphasizes Jesus' fulfillment of the Old Testament prophecies about the Messiah. Matthew's Jesus is more dignified and remote than Mark's. His sayings are gathered into several large sections, which alternate with accounts of His deeds. The Matthaean Jesus is not only concerned with the Jews: He commands His disciples to "teach all nations." This Gospel may have been written for a community of Jewish Christians in Syria. In the very beginning, the distinction between Jews and Christians was very vague. By now, however, the Jewish Christians were barred from the synagogues. To help them deal with their rejection by their brethren, the Gospel according to Matthew stressed that they were the true Israel (but one which did not exclude Gentiles).

Most of us picture Jesus the way Luke shows him: sensitive; compassionate; a friend of the poor, of sinners, outcasts and women. If the author of this Gospel was the Luke mentioned by Paul (and there is no strong reason against this identification), then he was a Gentile, the only non-Jewish author of any book of the Bible (cf. Col 4:10–14, where Luke is not included among the circumcised brethren). This Gospel and the Acts of the Apostles were written by the same person and originally were the two halves of a single work. Luke was a sensitive and conscientious writer. He addressed his Gospel to Gentiles, and often omitted material dealing with strictly Jewish matters. He includes a great deal of material (such as the accounts of the Prodigal Son, the Good Samaritan, and the Good Thief) not found in Matthew or Mark.

There is a persistent ambiguity about the titles given to Jesus in the Synoptic Gospels. In the first place, the intended meaning of such titles as "Son of God" or "Messiah" is unclear. Also, it is uncertain which titles were used by Jesus Himself and which were read back into His lifetime by the Gospel writers or their sources. Before considering these titles in greater detail, another unusual feature of the Synoptics should be noted. When the Synoptic Gospels were written, belief in Jesus' pre-existence and divine status (however unclearly expressed) was common in the early Church. This belief appears in Paul's letters, which were written much earlier; in fact, one of the clearest references is in an already existing Christian hymn that Paul quotes (Ph 2:6–11). It appears in the Gospel according to John, written a few decades later, and also in the Letter to the Hebrews, probably written around the same time as Matthew and Luke. Yet there is no clear reference to this in the Synoptics. Many of Jesus' actions in the Synoptics *imply* a divine status, but this is nowhere clearly affirmed. There is no mention of His pre-existence. If the Synoptics were all we had to go on, the natural conclusion would be that Jesus was a human being selected to be God's agent, who was raised to a semi-divine status after death. The answer to this problem may lie in the fact that the Gospels were not meant to be considered in isolation, out of the context of the teaching and practice of the early Church. We can safely say that the Synoptics guide and point the way, for the perceptive reader, to belief in Jesus' divinity.

  The following are the most significant titles given to Jesus in the Synoptics:

Son of God This is not used in the same sense as in the Gospel of John and the creeds of the Church. Sometimes it is used as a synonym for "Messiah" (cf. Lk 1:32). Luke connects the title to the Holy Spirit's role in the Virgin Birth (Lk 1:35). As normally used in the Synoptics, "Son of God" is ambiguous. Sometimes it virtually implies divine status (Mt 11:27); at other times it may only mean one who is favored by God (compare Mk 15:39 with Lk 23:47—Luke uses "innocent man" as a substitute for "Son of God"). Because it was intelligible to the Gentiles, this became the Church's favorite title for Jesus and soon took on the Trinitarian meaning it has today (cf. Mt 28:19, Jn 1:18, and Heb 1:1–4).

Son of Man In contrast, this title proved so unintelligible to non-Jews that it fell into practical disuse, even though it is the title Jesus usually gives to Himself in the Synoptics. There is a deliberate ambiguity in the use of this title. At one level, it is simply an Aramaic expression for "man." However, it is used in Daniel (7:13) and in the apocryphal Book of Enoch as the title of a God-like figure in heaven. In Mk 14:62, Jesus explicitly identifies Himself as both "Son of Man" and "Messiah," indicating that to Him they are synonymous. In this passage, he combines the passage from Daniel with the messianic Ps 110:1.

Messiah   To Jesus' contemporaries, the Messiah was the God-appointed successor of King David, predicted in Holy Scripture, who would save them from their foreign oppressors and usher in a golden age. Suetonius, Tacitus and Josephus all mention that the Jews at this time expected the Messiah to arrive shortly. Many people claiming to be the Messiah rose up in Palestine in this era, and tried to lead revolts against the Romans. They failed miserably, and only helped set the stage for the war which ended with the destruction of Jerusalem in 70 A.D. Jesus was very cautious about calling Himself the Messiah in front of the volatile crowds He preached to. At one point, according to Jn 6:15, He had to flee to avoid being named king by such a crowd. His conception of what "Messiah" truly meant was so different from the commonly accepted idea that He preferred to lead His disciples to the idea gradually (cf. Mt 16:13–23). At His trial, He admitted to the Jewish leaders that He was indeed the Messiah (Mk 14:62). "Christ" is the Greek equivalent of "Messiah"—both mean "anointed one." This title quickly became a synonym for "Jesus" in the early Church, and soon Jesus' followers were simply called "Christians" (Ac 11:26). As we have seen, this title was well known to the Roman and Jewish historians who mentioned Jesus.

The Testimony of the Gospel According to John

The basic structure of John's Gospel is like that of the Synoptics: it begins with Jesus' encounter with John the Baptist, describes His public ministry, crucifixion and death, and ends with His appearances to the disciples after the Resurrection. It describes some incidents—such as the cleansing of the Temple, the multiplication of the loaves, and the walking on the water—which are also found in the Synoptics, but most of its material is new.

What strikes the reader, however, is how *different* this Gospel is from the Synoptics. Jesus is shown throughout as the incarnate Son of God, God Himself. He speaks in long discourses, with many repetitions and double meanings. He Himself, not the Kingdom of God, is the subject of His preaching. He performs incredible feats—such as the raising of Lazarus from the dead—which are not even hinted at in the Synoptics.

What is the solution to this problem? How is John related to the Synoptics? Which gives the more accurate picture of Jesus? The Church has been aware of this tension from the start. John's Gospel was written sometime around 90–100 A.D. Within a hundred years, it had been so widely accepted that St. Irenaeus held it as axiomatic that there could only be four genuine Gospels. Some ancient writers held that John's Gospel was written to supplement the Synoptic accounts. While there may be an element of truth in this, the actual state of affairs, as reconstructed by modern scholars, is more complex.

This Gospel seems to come from a Christian community, connected with the apostle John, which by 100 A.D. was centered in Ephesus although it had strong roots in Palestine. This close-knit community tended to keep to itself, and it combined traditions about Jesus not found in the Synoptics with its own theological ideas about the Church and Jesus' divinity—ideas parallel to those held in the rest of the Church, but expressed in different language. Eventually, this community came into closer contact with the rest of the Church, and introduced them to its unique version of the Gospel.

John's Gospel tells us that it is a *document of faith*: it was written "to help you believe that Jesus is the Messiah, the Son of God, so that through this faith you may have life in his name" (Jn 20:31). It is also a *selective document*: "Jesus performed many other signs as well—signs not recorded here—in the presence of his disciples" (Jn 20:30). In John, to a great extent, the glory of Christ which was revealed after His departure by the Spirit is read back into His earthly life. At the same time, this Gospel reflects first-hand information about Palestine in the time of Jesus, and preserves traditions about Him that did not find their way into the Synoptics. Thus, we learn that Jesus conducted a baptizing ministry like John's, that He was active in Judea as well as in Galilee, that His public ministry lasted more than a year, that at one point crowds wanted to proclaim Him king, and that the Jewish authorities wanted Him executed because they were afraid that His messianic claims and the uproar they caused would provoke the Romans.

There are several key themes in John which that Gospel takes up again and again. Here are some of the most important:

Jesus' divinity and pre-existence   The opening lines of the Gospel are: "In the beginning was the Word, and the Word was with God, and the Word was God. He was with God in the beginning" (Jn 1:1–2). Jesus is "God the only Son, ever at the Father's side" (Jn 1:18). He is attacked for making Himself God's equal (Jn 5:18); He tells His audience that "Before Abraham was, I am" (Jn 8:58); He asks the Father for the "glory I had with you before the world began" (Jn 17:5); finally, Thomas calls Him "my Lord and my God" (Jn 20:28).

The gift of eternal life   Jesus sums up His message as follows: "I am the resurrection and the life: whoever believes in me, though he should die, will come to life; and whoever is alive and believes in me will never die" (Jn 11:25–26). This message is repeated throughout the Gospel in many different ways: cf. Jn 3:16, 36; 4:14; 5:24, 29; 8:32, 51, etc. Although John does not mention the institution of the Eucharist, the discourse on the Bread of Life (Jn 6:25–59) clearly refers to that sacrament. In John's thought, the sacraments are bonds of love that unite Jesus and the believer, as close as the bond between a vine and its branches (Jn 15:5).

Love   The theme of love pervades John's Gospel: the Father loves the Son (Jn 3:35); Jesus loves His disciples (Jn 13:1); they, in turn, must love one another (Jn 13:34–35).

The Paraclete   Another divine Person, beside the Father and the

Son, is presented in this Gospel. This is the Spirit, the Paraclete or advocate of the believing community. He is the Spirit of Truth (Jn 14:17; 15:26; 16:13); He is sent by the Father and the Son (Jn 15:26) to dwell in the Church (Jn 14:17) and remind the believers of all that Jesus told them, to guide and preserve them in the truth (Jn 14:26; 16:13). The Spirit's coming is delayed until after Jesus' earthly life (Jn 7:39; 16:7); Jesus imparts Him to the disciples after the Resurrection (Jn 20:22).

The Testimony of the Acts of the Apostles

As already mentioned, the Acts of the Apostles is the continuation of the Gospel according to Luke. It was written to show how the disciples carried out the risen Christ's command "to be my witnesses in Jerusalem, throughout Judea and Samaria, yes, even to the ends of the earth" (Ac 1:8). It is a selective history of the first few decades of the Church, concentrating on the spread of the Gospel message from the Jews to the Gentiles, and from Judea to Rome. It devotes much space to the work of Peter and Paul; the other early Church leaders receive little or no attention.

Acts has been called "the Gospel of the Holy Spirit." In a sense, this is true: from the descent at Pentecost (Ac 2:1–4), the Spirit is shown as guiding the Church at each step. But the activity of the Spirit cannot be understood apart from Jesus. Working through the Spirit, He is present throughout Acts.

The basic facts of Jesus' career are mentioned in several speeches in Acts (Ac 2:22–36; 3:12–26; 5:30–32; 10:37–43; 13:23–31); historically, this kind of oral presentation formed the backbone of the Gospels. But in Acts, He is not only the subject of preaching: He is present in the community of the faithful, living and active.

"Jesus must remain in heaven until the time of universal restoration" (Ac 3:21); "Exalted at God's right hand, he first received the promised Holy Spirit from the Father, then poured this Spirit out on us" (Ac 2:33); He is "the one set apart by God as judge of the living and the dead" (Ac 10:42).

Through His disciples, Jesus continues to heal people (Ac 3:6; 9:34; 16:18); He appears in visions (Ac 9:10–19; 18:9–10; 22:17–21), the greatest of which is the apparition that converts Saul (Ac 9:3–9). He is so closely identified with His followers that to persecute them is to persecute Him (Ac 9:4–5).

Many titles are given to Jesus in Acts: Messiah, Son of Man, Lord, Son of God, Savior, Servant, Just One, and Author of Life. The heart of the apostles' message is that Jesus is the Savior, that forgiveness is found only in His name (Ac 2:38; 4:12; 10:43).

The Testimony of St. Paul

St. Paul is without doubt the most important Christian writer who has ever lived. After Jesus Christ, he has influenced Christianity more than any other person. Besides his own direct influence through his writings, he was the decisive influence on two other Christian titans, St. Augustine and Martin Luther.

Paul (also called Saul) was somewhat younger than Jesus. He was a Jew of the tribe of Benjamin (Rm 11:1), a Roman citizen (Ac 22:25–29), born in Tarsus but educated in Jerusalem (Ac 22:3). A young man at the time Stephen was martyred (Ac 7:58), he became a fanatical persecutor of Christianity until he was converted by a vision of Jesus (Ac 9:1–9). He met Peter and James the brother of Jesus (Gal 1:18–19). Before his death in Rome around 64 A.D., he made three great missionary trips through what are now Greece and Turkey and wrote several letters to various Christian congregations. These are the earliest writings in the New Testament, predating the Gospels by several decades. Paul's earliest surviving work, the First Epistle to the Thessalonians, was written about twenty years after the Crucifixion.

Paul's letters were addressed to people who were already Christians. He wrote them in response to specific problems, and so was not concerned about setting forth a complete account of everything the Church taught. He is concerned with Jesus living and active through the Spirit in the Church, and devotes little time to His earthly career. One of the few exceptions is an account of the Last Supper (1 Cor 11:23–25).

Space permits only a brief look at Paul's rich theological vision. He was convinced that God had chosen him to preach "the Gospel concerning his Son, who was descended from David according to the flesh but was made Son of God in power according to the spirit of holiness, by his resurrection from the dead: Jesus Christ our Lord" (Rm 1:3–4).

The heart of Paul's message is that "God was in Christ reconciling the world to himself" (2 Cor 5:19), that "all men are now undeservedly justified by the gift of God, through the redemption wrought in Christ Jesus" (Rm 3:24). The community of believers make up the body of Christ, in which no distinction is made between "Jew or Greek, slave or freeman, male or female" (Gal 3:28).

Paul's most common title for Jesus is "Lord," and in its context this title has divine overtones. For Paul, Jesus is "the image of the invisible God, the first-born of all creatures. In him everything in heaven and on earth was created" (Col 1:15–16). This is very much like the picture of Jesus given in John's Gospel, although the terminology is different. The most precise statement of the way the early Church saw Christ's cosmic role is found in the Letter to the Hebrews (long attributed to Paul; most scholars would agree with Origen that only God knows who wrote it, although a good case could be made for Paul's companion Apollos, cf. Ac 18:24–28). This Letter tells us of God's "Son, whom he has made heir of all things and through whom he first created the universe. This Son is the reflection of the Father's glory, the exact representation of the Father's being, and he sustains all things by his powerful word" (Heb 1:2–3). Although not written by Paul, this passage is in complete conformity with his thought.

Paul's letters enjoyed great authority from the very start. The pseudonymous Second Epistle of Peter, written some time after 100 A.D., already put his works on a par with "the rest of Scripture" (2 P 3:16).

The Testimony of the Pre-Nicene Church

The Church has always taught that Jesus Christ is both God and man. Many Christian writers witness to this in the centuries before the Council of Nicaea (325 A.D.) officially defined this belief.

We have seen how the New Testament called Jesus "God the only Son," "the image of the invisible God" and "the exact representation of the Father's being." Some early Christian writers, like the authors of the Synoptic Gospels, referred to Jesus in terms that implied His divinity, but did not state it in so many words. For example, the *Didache*, a church manual written around 100 A.D., calls Jesus the Son of God (16:4) and Lord (10:6), and says that God bestowed "knowledge and faith and immortality" (10:2) and "spiritual food and drink and life everlasting" (10:3) through Him. Similarly, Clement of Rome, in his very important *Letter to the Corinthians* (96 A.D.), says that "Jesus Christ was sent from God" (*1 Clem.* 42:1).

Other early writers explicitly referred to Christ's divinity. A sermon written around 150 A.D., and wrongly attributed to Clement, tells us that "we must think of Jesus Christ as of God" (*2 Clem.* 1:1).

When Ignatius of Antioch was being taken to Rome for martyrdom around 107 A.D., he wrote several letters stressing Christ's humanity and divinity. To the Ephesians, he wrote that "our God Jesus Christ was, according to God's dispensation, the fruit of Mary's womb, of the seed of David" (*Ep.* 18). To the Smyrnaeans, he said "I give glory to Jesus Christ, the God who has imbued you with such wisdom. . . . He was of the race of

David according to the flesh, and the Son of God by His will and power" (*Smyrn.* 1).

Justin Martyr, in his *First Apology* (155 A.D.), referred to "the Logos Himself, who assumed a human form and became man, and was called Jesus Christ" (*1 Apol.* 5). Tertullian, in his *Apology* (197 A.D.), says that Jesus was "uttered by God and begotten by this utterance, and is, therefore, called the Son of God and God on account of the unity of nature" (*Apol.* 21:11). Melito of Sardis, around 150 A.D., in his *Paschal Homily* said that Christ was "by nature God and man."

Athenagoras, in his *Embassy for the Christians* (180 A.D.), stated the teaching of the Church in very clear terms: "The Son of God is Word of the Father in thought and power. All things were made through Him and after His fashion. The Father and Son are one. The Son being in the Father and the Father in the Son by the powerful union of the Spirit . . . the Son . . . is the First-begotten of the Father. He did not indeed come to be, for God was from the beginning, being eternal mind, and had His Word within Himself, being from eternity possessed of a Word" (*Emb.* 10). Clement of Alexandria, in his *Christ the Educator* (190 A.D.), described Jesus as follows: "He is God the Word, who is in the bosom of the Father, and also at the right hand of the Father, with even the nature of God" (*Paed.* 1:2).

Around 240 A.D., an anonymous Christian appealed to the witness of both Church writers and the popular belief of the Church in defense of the divinity of Christ. His statement was preserved in the *Ecclesiastical History* of Eusebius of Caesarea (early 4th century): "I refer to the works of Justin and Miltiades and Tatian and Clement [of Alexandria] and many others in all of which Christ is treated as God. For who is ignorant of the books of Irenaeus and Melito and the rest, which proclaim Christ as God and man? And all the psalms and hymns written by faithful brethren from the beginning sing of Christ as the Word of God and treat him as God" (*E.H.* 5:28).

The Official Teaching of the Church

Three major Church Councils (Nicaea, Ephesus and Chalcedon) defined Christ's divinity and the relationship between His human and divine natures.

The Council of Nicaea (325 A.D.), attended by 300 bishops, defined the divinity of Christ in response to Arius, an Alexandrian priest. Arius held that even though Christ could be called "God," and "Son of God," and that the world had been created through Him and that He had existed with the Father before the creation of the world, that yet He was still a created being inferior to God the Father. There had been a time, however remotely in the past, when the Son had not existed. Arianism continued to be a strong movement for decades after the Council. Its strongest opponent was Athanasius, Bishop of Alexandria, who had attended the Council of Nicaea as a deacon.

The Creed drawn up at this Council is as follows (not to be confused with the Nicaeo-Constantinopolitan Creed, which is the "Nicene Creed" recited at Mass): "We believe in one God, the Father almighty, maker of all things visible and invisible. And in one Lord Jesus Christ, the Son of God, only-begotten, born of the Father, that is, of the substance of the Father, God of God, light of light, true God of true God, born, not made, of one substance with the Father, through whom were made all things in heaven and earth. Who for us men and our salvation came down, was incarnate and made man, and suffered, and rose again the third day, and ascended into the heavens, and will come to judge the living and the dead. And in the Holy Spirit. But those who say 'There was a time when he was not,' and 'Before he was born, he was not,' and 'that he was made out of nothing' or out of some other substance or essence, or that the Son of God is changeable or mutable, these the Catholic Church anathematizes."

The Council of Ephesus (431 A.D.) condemned Nestorius,

the Bishop of Constantinople. Concerned that people were confusing Christ's human nature with His divine nature, he taught that Mary could be called "Mother of Christ," but not "Mother of God." The approximately two hundred bishops who met at Ephesus issued this statement: "One and the same is the eternal Son of the Father and the Son of the Virgin Mary, born in time after the flesh; therefore, she may rightly be called Mother of God."

Nestorianism had over-stressed the distinction between Christ's human and divine natures. In an over-reaction to this, the heresy of Monophysitism arose, which under-stressed the distinction. It taught that the two natures had so joined that Christ had become a sort of human/divine hybrid.

The Council of Chalcedon (451 A.D.) condemned the Monophysites. This Council stated that "following the holy fathers, we all with one voice teach that it should be confessed that our Lord Jesus Christ is . . . truly God and truly man . . . of one substance with the Father as to his Godhead, and at the same time of one substance with us as regards his manhood . . . recognized in two natures, without confusion, without separation, not as parted into two persons, but one and the same Son."

Comment

Jesus is the founder of Christianity. We cannot understand the Jesus of history and the Jesus of faith unless we examine the past. We cannot be indifferent to any age—each contributed insights into His sayings.

The New Testament gives us various pictures of Christ. Matthew stresses the Jewishness of Jesus. Mark presents Jesus as the suffering Savior of all peoples. In Luke, the compassionate and gentle Jesus is portrayed. John speaks of the Word of God made visible in the person of Jesus. Paul, the apostle of the Gentiles, portrays Jesus as the Lord of both Jew and Gentile.

In response to the heresies that arose in the first centuries, the divinity and humanity of Jesus were dogmatically defined by the Councils (Nicaea, Ephesus, Chalcedon) of the Church. They defended the pure picture of Christ as presented in the New Testament.

The Creeds drawn up by these Councils express stages of growth of the Church. The *Dogmatic Constitution on the Church* (ch. 1 art. 8) of the Second Vatican Council says:

This is the unique Church of Christ which in the Creed we avow as one, holy, catholic, and apostolic. After His Resurrection our Savior handed her over to Peter to be shepherded, commissioning him and the other apostles to propagate and govern her. He set her up for all ages as "the pillar and mainstay of the truth." This Church, constituted and organized in the world as a society, subsists in the Catholic Church, which is governed by the successor of Peter and by the bishops in union with that successor, although many elements of sanctification and of truth can be found outside of her visible structure. These elements, however, as gifts properly belonging to the Church of Christ, possess an inner dynamism towards Catholic unity.

Just as Christ carried out the work of redemption in poverty and under oppression, so the Church is called to follow the same path in communicating to men the fruits of salvation. Christ Jesus, "though He was by nature God . . . emptied Himself, taking the nature of a slave" and "being rich, He became poor" for our sakes. Thus, although the Church needs human resources to carry out her mission, she is not set up to seek earthly glory, but to proclaim humility and self-sacrifice, even by her own example. Christ was sent by the Father "to bring good news to the poor, to heal the contrite of heart," "to seek and to save what was lost." Similarly, the Church encompasses with love all those who are afflicted with human weakness. Indeed, she recognizes in the poor and the suffering the likeness of her poor and suffering Founder. She does all she can to relieve their need and in them she strives to serve Christ. While Christ, "holy, innocent, undefiled" knew nothing of sin, but came to expiate the sins of the people, the Church, embracing sinners in her bosom, is at the same time holy and always in need of being purified, and incessantly pursues the path of penance and renewal.

Special Questions

What about Jesus' human knowledge?
Some Gospel passages indicate that Jesus was ignorant of some things: He had to ask who had touched Him in a crowd (Mk 5:30–33); He did not know the date of the end of the world (Mk 13:32) but believed that it would be in His own generation (Mk 13:30); He misquoted Scripture (Mk 2:26; Mt 23:35). Other passages, however, indicate that He was omniscient. Besides His claims to be the Messiah and the Son of God, the Gospels record incidents of His extraordinary knowledge (Mk 2:8; Jn 1:48; 4:16–18; 13:38; Mt 16:21).

This has been a much-debated question. Raymond Brown, a noted biblical scholar, believes that Jesus could have been ignorant of some things because of His humanity and that this does not detract from His divinity. It would be a necessary part of the Incarnation. Bernard Lonergan, a leading systematic theologian, believes that Jesus was conscious of His identity as the Messiah. Karl Rahner, one of the leading Catholic theologians of modern times, believes that Jesus' human knowledge developed gradually and that this applies as well to His self-awareness. Three respected Catholic scholars and theologians, and three different views. What is the answer?

In this life we may not know the answer with absolute certainty. Though Jesus' conscious, human knowledge almost by definition would have to be limited, His human understanding was nevertheless extraordinary. Though perhaps ignorant of certain facts, He was convinced of His unique relationship with the Father and spoke and acted with authority. Moreover, in the totality of His personhood, His divine nature would require that He have infinite knowledge. But the mechanics of how the human consciousness of Jesus interacts with His divine nature remains a mystery open to speculation. Some theologians are convinced that because of the hypostatic union of His human and divine natures, Jesus could not have been limited in what He knew. Other theologians argue that because Jesus was truly human in all things but sin (cf. Heb 4:14–15), His human knowledge would have to develop gradually and be finite in scope. Though there is no doubt that Jesus is the God-Man, there are still many things about Him that are freely debated among Catholic scholars.

What do Jews believe about Jesus?

There is no single Jewish belief about Jesus. Some Jews consider Him to have been a prophet after the manner of Isaiah or Jeremiah; others feel that Jesus and His movement were out of the mainstream of Judaism from the beginning.

Judaism is based on the belief in the uniqueness of God. The idea of a divine Person equal to God the Father is completely alien to it. Whatever the individual opinions of Jews about Jesus are, He has no place in Jewish worship and official religious teaching.

The well-known "Jews For Jesus" movement is not an exception to this. They believe that the antithesis between Jews and Christians is a false one, that the distinction is between Jews and Gentiles and that people from both backgrounds can and should become Christians. Like the first Christians—who were all Jews—they believe that Jesus as the Messiah is the fulfillment, not the destruction, of Judaism. The theology of the "Jews For Jesus" is the same as that of fundamentalist Protestants. They accept the New Testament as well as the Old, and believe in the divinity of Jesus. It must be said that the vast majority of Jews do not believe that this movement can be considered part of Judaism, but is simply another Christian sect.

Jewish-Christian relations through the centuries have been stormy. As General Titus knew, "the Christians had grown out of the Jews." Jesus and His disciples were Jews. The first Christian communities were made up exclusively of Jews. It took a divine revelation to convince Peter that Gentiles were acceptable to God (Ac 10).

Within a few decades, however, most Christians were Gentiles. Jewish Christians were considered as apostates by most other Jews. For several centuries, some small Jewish Christian groups remained in communion with the Church, but retained many Jewish customs. Other Jewish Christians, like the Ebionites, drifted into heresy.

Some Jews cooperated with the pagans in persecuting the Church. For their part, Christians persecuted the Jews, and, when they came to power, imposed many restrictions on them.

Today, serious efforts are being made to improve relations between Catholics (and other Christians) and Jews. Ecumenism—efforts toward reunion—is a term only properly used for the efforts of Christian groups to come together. There can be no question of union between different religions, such as between Christianity and Judaism. Through dialogue, though, Jews have come to a better understanding of the Christian position, Christians have become more aware of their Jewish roots, and bigotry and anti-semitism have been fought. Much good has been done by this, but much more remains for the future.

What do Moslems believe about Jesus?

Jesus is mentioned several times in the Moslem scriptures, the Koran. Like the Jews, Moslems believe in the absolute uniqueness of God, or Allah. For them, Jesus is a great prophet, a messenger of Allah who performed many miracles. Moslems believe in the Virgin Birth, holding that, though only human, Jesus was created by the direct will of Allah. They believe that Jesus has not yet died—that the Crucifixion was only an illusion. Jesus was taken up into Paradise, where He will remain until the end of the world, when He will kill the Antichrist, die and be resurrected by Allah.

Moslems believe that Christianity is a distortion of the teachings of Jesus—the worst distortion being His deification. In the Koran, Jesus is shown as denying that He ever considered Himself to be Allah's equal.

As with Judaism, there is no question of union between Moslems and Christians. For both sides, such union would be apostasy. However, dialogues between Catholics and Moslems have been held, seeking to clear away misunderstandings and find areas of mutual agreement.

What do we mean by "the Body and Blood of Christ"?

At the Last Supper, Jesus took bread and wine, declared that they were His Body and Blood, and commanded His disciples to do this in memory of Him. This is related in the Synoptics (Mt 26:26–28; Mk 14:22–24; Lk 22:14–20) and in St. Paul (1 Cor 11:23–26). John contains a discourse referring to the Eucharist (Jn 6:48–58), but does not refer to its institution. Roman Catholics, Eastern Orthodox, Lutherans and most Anglicans believe that after the consecration Jesus is truly present in the bread and wine, although they differ on their terminology. Most other Christian denominations believe that Jesus is present in a symbolic manner.

Catholics (and the other Churches with similar beliefs) hold that the scriptural accounts support their position, and that this is confirmed by the writings of several early Church Fathers.

In his *Letter to the Philadelphians* (107 A.D.), Ignatius of Antioch said: "Be zealous, then, in the observance of one Eucharist. For there is the one flesh of our Lord, Jesus Christ, and one chalice that brings union in His blood" (*Phil.* 4).

Justin Martyr, in his *First Apology* (155 A.D.), stated: "We receive this not as ordinary bread and ordinary drink, but just as our Savior Jesus Christ was incarnated by the word of God . . . the food which has been made the Eucharist . . . is both flesh and blood of that same incarnate Jesus" (*1 Apol.* 66).

Irenaeus of Lyons was one of the most important theologians

in the early Church. In his *Against Heresies* (*circa* 200 A.D.), he writes: ". . . the mingled cup and the manufactured bread receives the Word of God, and the Eucharist of the blood and the body of Christ is made . . ." (*A.H.* 5:2:3).

Augustine (*circa* 400 A.D.) said: "the bread which you see on the altar is sanctified by the word of God, the body of Christ; . . . what is in the chalice is sanctified by the word of God, the blood of Christ" (*Sermon* 227).

Through twenty centuries, the Catholic Church has upheld the belief in Christ's real presence in the Eucharist. In the *Constitution on the Liturgy*, the Second Vatican Council stated: "at the Last Supper, on the night when He was betrayed, our Savior instituted the Eucharistic Sacrifice of His Body and Blood. He did this in order to perpetuate the sacrifice of the Cross throughout the centuries until He should come again."

Discussion Questions

1. Why are the non-Christian sources on the historical existence of Jesus so important?
2. Briefly show the different faces of Jesus as illustrated in the Synoptic accounts.
3. Why is John's Gospel so different from the Synoptics?
4. Read and discuss the Acts of the Apostles.
5. What is the key value of Paul's letters?
6. Why was it necessary for Paul to write these letters to the different Christian communities?
7. What is the importance of early documents like the *Didache* for Christians today?
8. The Council of Nicaea (325 A.D.) codified what Christians believe. Explain why it is the most significant statement of the Church in its long history.
9. Several early heretics like Arius and Nestorius were priests. How could this be?

10. Explain the statement, "Creeds express stages of growth of the Church."
11. A class project: From other theological sources, show the different points of view about Jesus Christ which are held by various Protestant Churches.
12. General Councils of the Church were not held every century. But there were times when two General Councils were held in one century. Explain.

WE BELIEVE IN OUR SALVATION

Chapter Three

WE BELIEVE IN OUR SALVATION

The theme of salvation is a fundamental aspect of the revelation of God. This term describes the divine action of restoring mankind to its state of wholeness. Salvation is at the heart of Creation, the Incarnation, and the Redemption. To be saved is to be permanently united with God and His people.

Revelation shows that we were created to be the image and likeness of God. Because of sin, this image has been disfigured. How was it to be reformed? This can be answered in one word— grace. Grace has been defined in many ways. Perhaps the best definition is that it is God's gift of Himself. How it is manifested in different ways at different times is another question. And so, we say that God saves.

In the Hebrew language, the word "salvation" (yeshuah) means "to take (one) out of a tight spot, to rescue, help, deliver, save." In the Old Testament, the word is often used in a military sense: "to win a victory for someone." In this sense, a victorious leader in war is a "savior" and a victory in battle is called a "salvation." For example: "When they cry to the Lord because of oppressors He will send them a savior and will defend and deliver them" (Is 19:20); and "Thou [God] hast granted this deliverance by the hand of thy servant [Samson]" (Jg 14:18). Of course, God is the rescuer or savior in the sense that He uses people to achieve His purpose. Besides the salvation God gave His people as a whole, he also intervened in favor of individuals who called on Him for aid. In the same sense, the New Testament reflects God's continued saving action for all people through the coming of Jesus Christ. Therefore, Jesus completed salvation. He was, in His very person, Salvation.

The Testimony of the Old Testament

The Judeo-Christian message is one of good news, because it shows how God, out of love and mercy, saved mankind. This point becomes clear in the pages of the Bible. Because God is discovered in the actions of human beings, we come to the knowledge of Him by reflecting on the principal events of salvation history.

At the heart of the Hebrew faith is the covenant. The covenant (Gn 15:7f; 17:1–8) established Yahweh as ruler of the Israelites, and made them His chosen people. Yahweh demanded fidelity to His commandments and promised in return His blessings and protection. For the Hebrews, salvation is rooted in the covenant. If it was observed faithfully, then Yahweh's protection would be guaranteed.

In the Old Testament, the covenant is shown as being broken from time to time. Yet Yahweh restores and renews the covenant in various ways.

The most dramatic example of how the Israelites saw Yahweh's saving hand in history is the story of the Exodus from Egypt (told in the first fifteen chapters of the book of Exodus). Yahweh was called "He who saves Israel" (1 S 14:39); the Israelites knew themselves as "a people saved by Yahweh" (Dt 33:29).

The flight from Egypt, the establishment of the Davidic kingdom and the grandeur of Solomon did not put an end to Israel's troubles. From around 720 to 540 B.C., the Hebrews experienced the worst emotional, psychological and historical crisis in their long history. The Assyrians took the ten tribes of the northern Kingdom of Israel into exile, and they disappeared from history, absorbed into the people they came to live among. Their remnant left in Israel mingled with foreigners brought in by the Assyrians and eventually formed the distinctive Samaritan religion. Then the population of the southern Kingdom of Judah was taken into exile by the Babylonians, but they retained their identity and were able, under the Persians, to re-establish themselves in the land of Israel.

They were sustained in their hopes by prophets like Jeremiah, who wrote that Yahweh would not forget His people and would save them.

This is an oft-repeated prophetic theme. Jeremiah stated that "in Yahweh, our God, alone is the salvation of Israel" (Jr 3:23), and not in pagan gods (2:27f). He expected Yahweh not only to rescue him personally (15:20; 17·14), but also to establish the Messianic kingdom of right and justice (23:5–6). Hosea writes: "But I [Yahweh] will have pity on the house of Judah, and I will deliver them by the Lord their God" (Ho 1:7). Ezekiel speaks not only of political salvation, but also of Israel's deliverance from impurity, idolatry and apostasy (Ezk 36:29; 37:23).

The second half of the book of Isaiah links the hope of salvation with Yahweh's justice and redemption (Is 43:3, 11–14; 44:24; 47:3–4). For Isaiah, the object of this hope is not merely the liberation from exile (49:6), the punishment of Israel's oppressors (49:25f), and the restoration of their land (49:8) and its capital (52:9), but also the establishment of Yahweh's reign (52:7).

The Psalms also express Israel's hope of salvation: in victory over hostile foreign powers (Ps 76:6–7; 108:10), the repatriation of exiles (14:7), the restoration of Jerusalem and the other devastated cities of Judah (69:36), and deliverance from personal enemies (7:2; 12:6), illness (6:3) and misfortune (69:2). The psalmists clearly understand that repentance is the basis for a true hope of salvation.

Yahweh saved through human beings. The Judges of Israel were saviors (Jg 2:16; 6:36f; 12:3). The kings, such as Saul and David (1 S 11:1–15; 2 S 5:17–25), were instruments of deliverance. The prophets, like Jeremiah and Ezekiel, were great leaders who encouraged their people (Jr 30; Ezk 36).

The Israelites also believed that Yahweh saved them through

the powers of nature (as, for example, in the events of the Exodus). All through the Hebrew Bible, there is an assumption of Yahweh's absolute control of the entire visible universe. All things work ultimately for God's purpose.

The Testimony of the New Testament

For the Christian, Jesus Christ fulfills the Old Testament hope of salvation in the most striking, personal and universal fashion.

The salvation described in the Old Testament is extended to the Gentiles (1 Tm 2:4; 4:10; Lk 3:6; Jn 3:17; Ac 28:28). Jesus is "the savior of the world" (Jn 4:42), and only through Him can a person find salvation (Jn 10:9).

The New Testament and Salvation

The title of Savior is given to Jesus (Lk 2:11; Jn 4:42; Ac 5:31; Ep 5:23; Ph 3:20; 2 Tm 1:10; 1 Jn 4:14). His name, *Jesus* (the Greek version of *Yeshuah*) in fact means *salvation*. In the Old Testament the title "savior" is only given to God. It is extended to Jesus, as God's Son, in the New Testament. Every human being is of concern to Jesus. He is savior of all peoples.

Belief in Jesus is necessary for salvation (Lk 8:17; Ac 16:30f; Rm 10:9; 1 Cor 1:21). "The ones along the path are those who have heard; then the devil comes and takes away the word from their hearts that they may not believe and be saved" (Lk 8:12). To believe is to accept a promise with confidence. In a word, belief is a commitment. Throughout the Gospels, Jesus calls His apostles and disciples to a commitment to Himself and His ideas. Salvation is the key idea.

The great adversary of our salvation is Satan, the power of evil (Lk 8:12; Mt 12:22–30; Ac 26:18). Paul was sent to the

Gentiles "to open their eyes that they may turn from darkness to light and from the power of Satan to God . . ." (Ac 26:18). Obviously, Satan, the evil one, stands as an obstacle to humanity's salvation as planned by God. The New Testament often mentions this danger to salvation. Satan is called the prince of this world (Jn 12:31). He is the one who tempts Jesus (Mt 4:1). Satan tempts with evil designs (1 Cor 7:5) and seduces some of the faithful (1 Tm 5:15). Satan is the power of darkness as opposed to the power of light (Ac 26:18). Yet Jesus proclaims that Satan will be ultimately subdued by the power of God (Lk 10:18). Although there is controversy (among theologians) as to whether Satan is a person or a principle of evil, the normative teaching of the Church, strongly expressed some years ago by Pope Paul VI, is that Satan is indeed a person.

In the biblical world, physical illnesses were believed to be a punishment from God for one's sins. Although this concept is erroneous, the followers of Jesus (like their contemporaries) appeared to believe it (Jn 9:2). Jesus was capable of healing both body and soul (Lk 5:23–24). This inspired His followers and infuriated His enemies. Healing was a concrete sign of Jesus' saving power.

The Synoptic Gospels speak of healing as a means of salvation (Mt 9:21; Mk 3:4; Lk 6:9; 8:48; 17:19). A hemorrhaging woman saw Jesus and "said to herself, 'If I only touch his garment, I shall be made well'" (Mt 9:21).

We achieve salvation through the work of God's mercy and not by our own activity (Rm 3:23–24). It is a work of His grace (Ep 2:5) and His patience (2 P 3:15). In other words, work, without grace, does not merit God's salvation. God gives grace to every human being. Both Jews and Gentiles are saved through the grace of the Lord Jesus (cf. Ac 15:11; Rm 2:10). Grace is the favor of God. This doctrine is especially developed in the Pauline and Johannine writings. Paul stresses that Jesus brought salvation through His death and Resurrection. John sees the sending of the Son, Jesus, by God the Father as a grace. Whoever remains committed to Jesus does not lose His grace. Sin, by definition, is a free rejection of God's love.

Jesus confers salvation from sin. He gives repentance and forgiveness of sins (Ac 5:31). Without repentance, one cannot gain salvation. In the New Testament, sin is a failure to fulfill the will of God, and also a refusal to submit to Jesus. In the Old Testament, only God can deliver the individual or nation from sin. In the New Testament, He delivers the individual and the world from sin through, with, and in Jesus the Savior.

The Synoptic Gospels stress the forgiveness of sin. Luke says that the sinner need only ask forgiveness (18:9–14) and that joy will be obtained in heaven at the return of the sinner (15:7, 10). In John's writings, the malice of sin is emphasized. Sin is shown as the lust of the flesh, the lust of the eyes, and the pride of life (1 Jn 2:16). For Paul, Jesus is the conqueror of sin (Rm 6:9–10; 1 Cor 15:3; Gal 1:4).

Salvation is from the Jews (Jn 4:22), who are the channels of God's revelation. In his Letter to the Romans, Paul says, "So I ask, have they [the Jews] stumbled so as to fall? By no means. But through their trespass, salvation has come to the Gentiles" (Rm 11:11). Through the election of the Jews and the covenant with them, God prepared the world for His Son, Jesus Christ. Through them, He revealed Himself as the living and loving God. Through Christ, God unfolds His plans for humanity. The Hebrew prophets saw God's design in all events, even the catastrophic ones. In the days of the Exile and after, we see the Hebrews looking for a Messiah who will deliver them from their oppressors. Finally, Jesus comes as that promised Messiah. God's grace was with them from the days of Abraham, Moses, Joshua, Saul, David, Isaiah, Jeremiah, Ezekiel, Amos, Hosea and Micah, to Jesus. As the Letter to the Hebrews put it, "In times past, God spoke in fragmentary and varied ways to our fathers through the prophets; in this, the final age, He has spoken to us through His Son" (Heb 1:1-2).

Faith is the principle of salvation. However, faith without works (deeds) cannot save. The Letter of James says, "What does it profit, my brethren, if a man says he has faith, but has not works? Can his faith save him? . . . so, faith by itself, if it has no works, is dead" (Jm 2:14–17).

The sixteenth century Protestant reformer, Martin Luther, rejected the Letter of James because he stressed that faith alone was necessary for salvation. Later Lutherans, however, accepted James as canonical. In opposition to Luther, the Catholic Church taught that faith must be accompanied by works. It based this teaching on the passage from James just cited, and also from such passages as Jn 3:21 and Mt 25:31–46.

In actual fact, the Lutheran and Catholic positions on faith and works were never as far apart as might be supposed. The Lutherans never denied that good works were a consequence of faith. The Catholics never denied that faith came before works. In an official discussion held in Ratisbon in 1541, Cardinal Contarini and the representatives of the Lutheran Church reached substantial agreement on this issue, but their dialogue broke down on other issues. In our own day, although important differences remain, Lutherans and Catholics are moving toward a common consensus on this question.

Faith means "to believe," "to hold as trustworthy." Because Jesus performed many works, people believed. They considered Him trustworthy. Yet faith is more than an intellectual assent to the teachings of Jesus. By its nature, faith is inseparable from love and the demands of love. Jesus commands His followers "to love your neighbor." He gave a very graphic example, the parable of the Good Samaritan (Lk 10:25–37). The rigid distinction between faith and works is not in accord with the New Testament. The two go together.

The New Testament idea of salvation is in many ways most fully developed in the Gospel of Luke and the Acts of the Apostles. The signs and wonders worked by the apostles continued those of Jesus, the source of all salvation (Ac 2:43; 5:12).

The Official Teaching of the Church

The early Fathers of the Church, such as Cyprian, Ambrose and Augustine, believed in the universality of God's salvation. Although their writings are not binding dogmatic statements, they do indicate the thinking of the Church during the 3rd and 4th centuries.

The first official statement of the Church on this subject was made by the Council of Carthage (418). In the 6th century, the Second Council of Orange (526–530) said "The assistance of God ought to be implored always, even by those who have been reborn and have been healed, that they may arrive at a good end, or may be able to continue in good work" (Canon 10). This statement was issued against the followers of Pelagius (5th century) who believed that the beginning of faith depends solely on man's free will, although faith itself and its increase depend absolutely upon God. They also held that final perseverance is not a special gift of grace, but depends on man's own strength.

Another dogmatic statement on God's salvation was made at the Council of Trent (1545–1563) at its sixth session (1547). It stated that the justified without the special help of God cannot persist in the justification received. This was directed against the ideas on predestination held by the Calvinists.

Pope Innocent X (1653) condemned a statement of Cornelius Jansen, who claimed that God does not give the grace required to keep some of His commandments. Pope Clement XI (1713) condemned the Jansenist claim that "without grace, we can do nothing, but what tends to our condemnation." The First Vatican Council (1869–1870) reiterated the Second Council of Orange's statement that faith is a gift from God and that its action is at work pertaining to salvation.

In our own time, the Second Vatican Council (1962-1965) stressed the importance of the role of God's salvation in history. These statements are contained in two documents: the *Dogmatic Constitution on the Church* (#2-4, 9) and the *Dogmatic Constitu-*

tion on Divine Revelation (#2–4). The *Dogmatic Constitution on the Church* formed the theological basis for the other documents. It declared that: "At all times and among every people, God has given welcome to whosoever fears Him and does what is right (cf. Ac 10:35). It has pleased God, however, to make men holy and save them not merely as individuals without any mutual bonds, but by making them into a single people . . ." (9).

The *Dogmatic Constitution on Divine Revelation* stressed that God has revealed Himself to all peoples throughout history, and that His definitive revelation is in Jesus Christ. He is the one source of all revelation, in whichever form—in the Bible and tradition—the Church has handed it down.

The Church officially teaches that Jesus died for all people. All receive sufficient grace to avoid sin and can attain salvation. It would be a heresy to say that Jesus died only for the predestined or only for believers. It would be equally dangerous to say that pagans, heretics, etc., do not receive any sufficient grace.

Comment

There are thousands of books on the history of man's religions. They record the beliefs, symbols, legends and rituals of all peoples. These have a common theme—the notion of salvation.

Two points stand out clearly in this material: that people are imperfect and that they need outside help. A few examples will illustrate this:

1. The Navaho Indians of the Southwest believe in the power of their gods. They worship them in distinctive ceremonies in order to gain their protection.
2. The ancient Sumerians, Assyrians and Babylonians worshipped a number of gods, especially Marduk, who was thought to reward them with his blessings.
3. The Egyptians were very concerned about death and the af-

terlife. In their burial chambers, they provided for other neces-
sities for their continued life in another world.
4. Similarly, the Greeks and Romans were careful about which
gods they should sacrifice to and how to do it. The Greek
"mystery" religions had a concept of salvation similar in
some ways to that of the Christians. They believed their
secret rituals would unite the believer to their god, and confer
bliss and immortality on him.
5. The aim of the Hindus is to reach oneness with God, whom
they believe may be considered either as personal or impersonal. The doctrine of reincarnation is fundamental for them.
People are believed to have to return again and again to this
world to work out their perfection. The Buddhists hold similar
beliefs, but their ultimate value, whether it be called *Nirvana*
or *Dharma* or *Moksha*, could only be called "God" in a very
inaccurate sense.
6. Finally, Judaism, Christianity and Islam explicitly hold the
idea of the individual's salvation.

Therefore, salvation is the distinctive, inclusive and essential
theme of all religions. Salvation delivers the believer from es-
trangement from the gods or God, and restores both parties to
their proper relationship.

The process of salvation can be divided into three major
aspects: the faults to be conquered; the means to do this; and
restoration of the proper relationship with God.

In Jewish belief, Yahweh saves by His power, often through
human means. In the Hebrew Bible, His most magnificent saving
act is His deliverance of Israel out of Egypt (the Exodus). During
the Babylonian Exile and the Post-Exilic period, the Jewish concept of God's power deepened and became more universal. Salvation came to mean the promise of a future redemption, both
national and personal. Christianity sees this redemption realized
in the person of Jesus. In Christian belief, Jesus' Incarnation,
death and Resurrection mean salvation. It is the divinely estab-

lished way of liberation from sin and reconciliation with God. God's grace, of course, has always been available as an unearned gift of love. We can only respond to the gift of grace. Salvation is an act of God's love.

Special Questions

Can non-Christians be saved?

Clearly, non-Christians can be saved, and are saved. This positive answer rests on the notion of grace. Grace is God's total and complete presence, even though it may be revealed in many different ways at different times. It has always existed and been available; therefore, the primitive and ancient peoples, who did not know Jesus and the one God, certainly experienced God's grace. Their salvation depended, like that of all of us, on their response to it. Obviously, they had to deal with this in light of their knowledge and experience.

The ancient non-Christian religions of the Egyptians, Greeks, Romans, etc., all had some sense of divinity, some practice of worship and morality, and some belief in an afterlife. They ranged from polytheism to monotheism, and every shade of belief in between. Some modern non-Christian religions, such as Zoroastrianism, Islam, and Judaism, believe in one God. Hinduism is both polytheistic and monotheistic. It worships many gods, but sees them all as aspects of the one God, called Brahman. Buddhism holds to the belief in a state of ultimate liberation, enlightenment and bliss, called Nirvana. Buddhism may be called a non-theistic religion. Taoism is directed to the perception of the ultimate principle of the universe, called the Tao. Shintoism is an extremely archaic Japanese religion, based on polytheism and nature worship.

Judaism has always had a special relationship with Christianity for obvious historical and theological reasons. Christianity came out of Judaism; as Pope Pius XI once said, "Spiritually, we are all Semites." The Jews are still the covenant people; they were never (contrary to what some Christians have said) abandoned by God; Jesus came from them; they (as well as others) are called to the final Kingdom of God.

Father Richard McBrien, the noted theologian, said it well: "God is available to all peoples widely differentiated as they are by time, by geography, by culture, by language, by temperament, by social and economic conditions, etc. Revelation is received according to the mode of the receiver and the response to revelation (religion) is necessarily shaped by that mode of reception."

The official teaching of the Church on the question of the salvation of non-Christians was clearly stated in some of the documents of the Second Vatican Council (1962–1965):

1. The *Dogmatic Constitution on the Church* (#16): "Those also can attain everlasting salvation, who, through no fault of their own, do not know the gospel of Christ or His Church, yet sincerely seek God and are moved by grace to strive by their deeds to do His will as it is known to them through the dictates of conscience. Nor does divine Providence deny the help necessary for salvation to those who, without blame on their part, have not yet arrived at an explicit knowledge of God, but who strive to live a good life, thanks to His grace."

2. The *Declaration on the Relationship of the Church to non-Christian Religions* (#2): "The Catholic Church rejects nothing which is true and holy in these religions."

And so, the non-Christian can be saved. Christians are reminded that since grace exists in these groups, we must respect their freedom and work with them on projects of mutual concern.

Will the world end soon?

Every generation asks this question. One's own time always appears to be worse than that of the past generation. Moral decadence, wars, natural disasters, crimes, etc., all provoke this question. Some people fear that the world will end soon in a triumph of evil over good, in some disaster such as a nuclear holocaust.

This question is linked with three others: the problem of nuclear weapons; the justice of God; and the interpretation of biblical prophecies.

We are well aware that, for the first time in history, the total destruction of the world is possible. With nuclear weapons, we seem uncomfortably near the brink of destruction. Will it happen? When? How? Plagued by these questions, many people think that the end of the world is at hand.

Some people believe that the world will end soon because of God's justice. Although the treatment of "justice" in the Bible is complex and nuanced, the clear sense emerges that it is bound to the covenant and to God's righteousness. God's judgment was seen as both vindictive (Jos 7:1–26) and corrective (Ezk 5:7–17; Dt 7:9–11). In the New Testament also, the judgment of God is associated with condemnation (Mt 5:22; Lk 12:58; Jn 3:18; Rm 5:16). Thus, some people fear that God's justice will demand that He end the world because of the many violations of His laws.

This fear is confirmed for some people by their reading of the various biblical prophecies. For the Israelites, fire was the element Yahweh used to destroy the wicked: Sodom and Gomorrah (Gn 19:24); Israel's enemies (Am 1:4f); the wicked in general (Is 1:31; Ezk 22:17–22).

This notion was continued in the New Testament. John the Baptist spoke of a fiery judgment (Mt 3:10; Lk 3:9); so did Jesus: "when Lot went out from Sodom fire and brimstone rained from heaven and destroyed them all . . . so will it be on the day when the Son of Man is revealed" (Lk 17:29–30). As the Second Letter of Peter puts it: "The day of the Lord will come like a thief, and on that day the heavens will vanish with a roar; the elements will be destroyed by fire" (2 P 3:10). The Book of Revelation (the Apocalypse) speaks of the end of this world in striking terms.

What can we say about all of this? These prophecies were

written in symbolic language, not always easy for us to understand. They were not intended to be predictions of what is happening today, in spite of the interpretations of many Christian fundamentalists.

We do not know when the world will end. As Jesus Himself said, "No one knows the day or the hour, not the angels, not even the Son, only the Father" (Mk 13:32).

Instead of asking "When will the world end?" it might be better to ask "How can we create a better world with our God-given talents?"

Discussion Questions

1. Why is salvation the key doctrine of Christianity?
2. Read and discuss chapters 1 to 15 of Exodus.
3. Jeremiah has been called the prophet of salvation. Read Jr 3:11–4:4; 30:1–31:40; 33:1–26 and discuss this idea.
4. Yahweh saved through human means in the Old Testament. Give examples.
5. Read the Book of Jonah (it is very short). How did God and Jonah disagree about the salvation of the Ninevites (Gentiles)?
6. Read the following on the power of evil and discuss: Mt 12:22–30; Lk 8:12; Ac 26:17–18.
7. Do you think Satan is a person, or an impersonal principle of evil? Discuss and give reasons.
8. Why is salvation connected with the notion of healing?
9. Why, for our salvation, was it necessary for Jesus to be born as a man, die, and rise from the dead? Read Gal 4:1–7 and discuss.
10. Read the following on Jesus' conquest of sin: Rm 7:1–25; 1 Cor 15:3; Gal 1:4. Discuss.
11. What is wrong with the idea of predestination?
12. In your own life, can you give examples of God's continuing saving action?

WE BELIEVE IN THE HOLY SPIRIT

THE TESTIMONY OF THE OLD TESTAMENT

THE TESTIMONY OF THE NEW TESTAMENT

THE OFFICIAL TEACHING OF THE CHURCH

COMMENT

SPECIAL QUESTIONS

WHAT ABOUT THE "GIFT OF TONGUES"?

WHAT IS THE CHARISMATIC MOVEMENT?

DISCUSSION QUESTIONS

Chapter Four

WE BELIEVE IN THE HOLY SPIRIT

The Church's teaching on the Holy Spirit (Holy Ghost) as the third Person of the Trinity developed gradually in the Bible and in the writings of the Fathers. When we speak of the Trinity, we must use our language carefully. There is only one God; on that, Jews, Moslems and Christians are agreed. But Christians hold that this one God is eternally existent in three divine Persons. The Spirit is God. He is distinct from God the Father and God the Son. Yet there is only one God. We cannot adequately explain the Trinity. It is a divine mystery which the Church accepts on faith. From the very beginning, the Church has attributed different roles to the different divine Persons. In the first century, for example, Paul wrote to the Corinthians: "The grace of the Lord Jesus Christ, and the love of God, and the fellowship of the Holy Spirit be with you all" (2 Cor 13:13). We can phrase it another way: God the Father loves us; He reconciles us to Himself by giving us His Son (Jesus) made man and He lives in us by the Spirit of His love.

The Testimony of the Old Testament

The Old Testament speaks many times of the Spirit of God. In Hebrew, "spirit" means "breath" or "wind." The phrase is used to indicate the divine power at work in the world. It did not mean a divine Person distinct from God the Father. In order to understand this point, let us see how the Old Testament speaks of the Spirit of God. We can divide its treatment into five categories:

First, the Spirit of God is the source of life. Job says that he will not speak falsehood "as long as my breath is in me and the Spirit of God is in my nostrils" (Jb 27:3). In Genesis, Adam is brought to life by God's breath (Gn 2:7).

Second, the Spirit of God gives strength and courage. Men like Moses, Joshua, Gideon, Samson, and Saul perform extraordinary deeds of heroism. This was often expressed in colorful terms. For example, the Book of Judges says that Samson "found a fresh jawbone of an ass, and put out his hand and seized it, and with it he slew a thousand men" (Jg 15:15).

Third, the Spirit of God acts as a moral force. Isaiah speaks of the Spirit of God resting on His servant to make him a light to the nations (Is 42:1–6). Also the Spirit of God rests on the prophet who announces the good news of salvation and justice (Is 61:1–3). This idea also appears in Jeremiah and Ezekiel (Jr 31:31–34; Ezk 36:26–28).

Fourth, the Spirit is instrumental in the work of salvation (Ps 51:12–14).

Fifth, the Spirit is reflected in various images, such as fire (Dt 4:24; 9:10), wind (Nb 11:31; Ex 15:8) and water (Ps 42:1–3).

As already mentioned, the authors of the Old Testament did not conceive of the Holy Spirit as being a Person. They saw the Spirit, like the Word, or Wisdom, as being part of God and yet distinct in a mysterious manner. Using many striking poetic images to express their understanding of God's work, they laid the foundation for the Christian doctrine of the Trinity.

The Testimony of the New Testament

The New Testament, like the Old, speaks of the Spirit of God as coming down from on high. He is "poured out" (Ac 10:44–45) and "sent" by the Father (Gal 4:6). However, the New Testament introduces the idea that the Spirit is a Person and not simply an impersonal aspect of God. The Spirit does not appear very often in Matthew and Mark. He plays a prominent part in

Luke/Acts, although here it is not always clear whether the Spirit is understood as being personal or impersonal. The idea of the personality of the Spirit comes out clearly in John, and also in Paul.

Luke's Gospel often speaks of the Spirit's power: in Elizabeth's conception of John (1:15); in Mary's conception of Jesus (1:35); in Jesus' experience in the desert (4:1); in His public ministry (4:14). The Father gives the Spirit in answer to prayer (11:13); Jesus rejoices in the Spirit (10:21); He sends the Spirit on his disciples (24:49).

In John's Gospel the Spirit figures as the counselor (Paraclete), the Spirit of Truth (14:17; 15:26; 16:13). The Spirit teaches the faithful (14:26) and convicts the world of sin (16:8–11). The word "Paraclete" only appears in John. Most biblical scholars agree that the word is used in an active sense—that is, as "intercessor" or "helper" rather than "comforter" or "consoler." It is not so much a title as a term specifying a certain function of the Holy Spirit. John stresses the role of the Paraclete in the divine judgment. The Holy Spirit therefore is seen as intercessor, advocate, witness for the defense. Christ tells His disciples that the world would hate them, but that they need not worry; the Spirit will bear witness on His behalf (Jn 15:26).

The Spirit's role as guardian and protector emerges clearly in connection with the Judgment (Jn 14:16-17; 15:26; 16:13). Jesus, while He was on earth, was the shepherd (protector) (Jn 17:12). Now, however, the Father sends the Holy Spirit at Jesus' request (Jn 14:16), to be His replacement (Jn 14:26). The Holy Spirit brings no new teaching, but rather a fuller insight into the revelation of Christ.

As already mentioned, Acts has been called "the Gospel of the Holy Spirit." The Spirit, sent by Jesus from the Father (Ac 2:33), guides the early Church at each step. The apostles are transformed (2:3f); taught what to say (2:18); and encouraged (9:31).

Paul vividly describes the Spirit's divine, dynamic force. Christ gave us a covenant of the Spirit (2 Cor 3:8); the Spirit will raise us from the dead (Rm 8:11); the Spirit dwells in believers, making them temples of God (1 Cor 3:16). We are saved through the Spirit (Gal 5:25), and the Spirit awakens love in us (Col 1:8). "The Lord is the Spirit, and where the Spirit of the Lord is, there is freedom. All of us, gazing on the Lord's glory with unveiled faces, are being transformed from glory to glory into his very image by the Lord who is the Spirit" (2 Cor 3:17–18).

Paul knew, from his Jewish heritage, that the Spirit gave the prophets insight into hidden things (Dn 13:45; Si 48:24–25), and produced extraordinary phenomena, ecstasy and prophetic visions, heroic deeds, strength and inspiration.

After his conversion, Paul came to an understanding of the personality of the Holy Spirit. In writing his letters, he obviously was not concerned about writing exhaustive and complete creeds and dogmatic statements. His goal was to share his experience of the Spirit with his readers. Therefore, his references to the Spirit often leave it unclear whether he is speaking of a force or a Person. In some passages, he is clearly speaking of a Person (Rm 8:16, 26; 1 Cor 12:11; 2 Cor 3:17–18).

The Synoptic Gospels do not explicitly speak of the Spirit as a personality. An exception is Mt 28:19, "Go therefore and make disciples of all nations, baptizing them in the name of the Father, and of the Son, and of the Holy Spirit." The same is generally true of Acts, but this book contains several passages which make no sense unless the Spirit is considered as a Person. Ac 5:3–4 equates lying to the Spirit with lying to God. In Ac 8:29; 13:2; 21:11; 28:25 the Spirit is shown as speaking. The personality of the Spirit is also implied in Ac 15:28, where the apostles, having set the conditions for Gentile membership in the Church, state that "it has seemed good to the Holy Spirit and to us to lay upon you no greater burden than these necessary things."

In his Gospel, John refers to the Spirit as a Person several times. The Spirit will remain with the Church (14:16–17) and remind Jesus' followers of all that He said (14:26; 16:13–14). The Spirit is sent by Jesus from the Father (15:26) after Jesus' earthly career is over (16:7). He bears witness for Jesus (15:26) and convicts the world of sin (16:8–11).

The Old Testament speaks of the power of the Spirit but not of the plurality of Persons in God. In the New Testament, the revelation of the Spirit as a distinct Person is clear. It was on this Scriptural foundation (and under the guidance of the Holy Spirit) that the Church formulated her teachings on the divinity and personality of the Spirit.

The Official Teaching of the Church

Several early Christian writers mentioned the personality and divinity of the Holy Spirit. Clement of Rome (1st century) and Ignatius of Antioch (2nd century) refer to the Spirit's divinity. Tertullian (3rd century) said that the Holy Spirit proceeds from the Father through the Son. Athanasius (4th century) said that the Holy Spirit is equal to the Father and the Son. Basil, Gregory of Nazianzen and Gregory of Nyssa stressed that the Holy Spirit proceeds from the Father and is not begotten as is the Son. John Damascene (8th century) stressed the Spirit's equality with the Father and the Son. These Fathers give us a clear picture of the beliefs of the early Church about the Holy Spirit.

Eventually, the personality and divinity of the Holy Spirit was officially defined by the Church in her Councils.

The First Council of Constantinople (381) proclaimed its belief "in the Holy Spirit, the Lord and giver of life who proceeds from the Father, who together with the Father and Son is worshipped and glorified." This Council made explicit the Holy Spirit's procession from the other two divine Persons. The First General Council of Nicaea (325) had defined the Trinitarian belief of three Persons in one God. But it was more concerned with the relationship between the Father and the Son.

The First Council of Constantinople also condemned the heresies of Macedonius and Apollinaris. Macedonius denied the divinity of the Holy Spirit. Apollinaris believed that Jesus had a human body but no human mind or human soul. In other words, that Christ was truly God but not truly man.

The Council of Rome (382) stated that there are three true Persons in God: the Father, and the Son, and the Holy Spirit; all are equal and immortal. This provincial Council was summoned by Pope Damasus in Rome to reaffirm what was stated at Constantinople a year before. He had not been present at this General Council, and some scholars feel that he summoned his own Council as a gesture of support and approval.

The Eleventh Council of Toledo (675) said: "We also believe that the Holy Spirit, the Third Person in the Trinity, is God, and that He is one and equal with God the Father and God the Son, of one substance as well as one nature. However, He is not begotten or created, but He proceeds from both and is the Spirit of both." Note that this Council stated that the Spirit proceeds from both the Father and the Son. This is the concept that prevailed in the Western Church. The teaching of the Eastern Church is that the Spirit proceeds from the Father through the Son. Eventually, an addition was made in the West to the Creed expressing the distinctive local belief. This addition (the so-called *filioque*— the statement that the Spirit proceeds from the Son as well as the Father) was rejected by the Eastern Church. Through the centuries, this has been a cause of bitterness and division between these Churches.

The Fourth Lateran General Council (1215) stated: "We firmly believe and simply confess that there is only one true God, eternal, immense, unchangeable, incomprehensible, omnipotent, and ineffable, the Father, the Son, and the Holy Spirit, three Persons but one essence, substance or wholly simple nature."

This statement was directed against the Albigensians, who believed in two Gods, one good and one evil, and who also denied the Trinity, Incarnation, Redemption and Sacraments.

The Second Council of Lyons (1274) stated: "And we believe that the Holy Spirit, completely and perfectly true God, proceeding from the Father and from the Son is co-equal, co-substantial, co-omnipotent and co-eternal with the Father and the Son in all things." This Council tried to heal the schism between the Eastern and Western Churches, already two centuries old. It taught the Western doctrine of the procession of the Holy Spirit. Not surprisingly, it failed to end the breach with the Eastern Church.

The General Council of Florence (1439–1445) carefully taught the distinction of one divine Person from another. It stated: "The Holy Spirit alone proceeds both from the Father and equally from the Son. These three Persons are one God, not three Gods; for the three Persons have one substance, one essence, one nature, one divinity, one immensity, one eternity." This Council also tried to heal the Eastern–Western schism. After much debate, the Greek delegates from Constantinople agreed that the *filioque* was a legitimate addition to the Creed. For a while, it looked as if East and West were once more united. It soon became clear, however, that the Eastern Church as a whole rejected this agreement.

Later, the Council of Trent (1545–1563) and the First Vatican Council (1869–1870) had to deal with other problems about God. The Council of Trent defended, against the Reformers, the idea that God does not deliberately and explicitly exclude some people from salvation. The First Vatican Council rejected pantheism.

The Conciliar teaching is, in summary: the Holy Spirit is God; He is not begotten but proceeds both from the Father and the Son. It is an open question to what extent the Eastern and Western formulations, beneath their difference in language, are describing the same concept of the Holy Spirit's procession.

Comment

We have always believed that the Holy Spirit is true God, a distinct Person of the Trinity, one substance with the Father and the Son, eternal, equal to the other two divine Persons. Such is the profession of the Athanasian and Nicaeo-Constantinopolitan Creeds, both of the 4th century.

During the first seven centuries, the Church had not clearly formulated the exact manner and source of the Holy Spirit's procession, and the exact role of the Son in this. In the Western Church, the statement that the Spirit proceeds from both the Father and the Son became generally accepted and was added to the Creed.

The first Christians of apostolic times had a practical, not metaphysical, understanding of the Holy Spirit and His works. The Spirit speaks to, guides, influences and dwells in the Christian. They experienced His power. In the baptismal rite, from the beginning, the Spirit was mentioned together with the Father and the Son, implying a common divinity (cf. Mt 28:19).

Through the first centuries, the Church Fathers developed new insights into the divinity, procession and personality of the Holy Spirit, and His relationship with the Father and the Son. While East and West differed on the question of the Holy Spirit's procession, there was and is general agreement on the basics. The Church's understanding of the Spirit—in her liturgical life, the devotions of her people and the insights of her theologians— deepens over the centuries. This process is guided by the Holy Spirit.

The Second Vatican Council's *Dogmatic Constitution on the Church* expressed it well: "When the work which the Father had given the Son to do on earth was accomplished, the Holy Spirit was sent on the day of Pentecost in order that He might forever sanctify the Church, and thus all believers would have access to the Father through Christ in one Spirit. . . . Thus, the Church shines forth as a people made one with the unity of the Father, the Son, and the Holy Spirit." (#4)

Special Questions

What about the "Gift of Tongues"?

In his First Letter to the Corinthians, Paul mentions the various gifts of the Holy Spirit. These are wisdom, knowledge, faith, healing, miraculous powers, prophecy, spiritual discernment, tongues, and the interpretation of tongues (1 Cor 12:4–11). The gift of tongues (also called glossolalia) was common in the early Church, and today is common in Pentecostal and Charismatic groups. A person with this gift can praise God in a language not know to him or her. In most cases, this is not related to any earthly language. It is a debated point among theologians and psychologists as to whether this type of speech can be considered a language, or whether it is simply a meaningless succession of sounds. Some Charismatics have reported speaking in tongues that turned out to be languages unknown to them, such as Greek or Japanese. At present, the evidence for this is too fragmentary and unverified for a proper evaluation.

Whatever the exact nature of this gift, the first Christians saw it as a Spirit-derived way to praise God. It is mentioned several times in the New Testament. In Mk 16:17, Jesus is represented as saying, "Those who believe in my name, they will cast out demons; they will speak in new tongues." At Pentecost, the Spirit descended on the apostles. "All were filled with the Holy Spirit. They began to express themselves in foreign tongues and make bold proclamations as the Spirit prompted them" (Ac 2:4). Acts mentions similar events a number of times: "they heard them speaking in tongues and extolling God" (10:46); "they spoke with tongues and prophesied" (19:6).

Paul made the best evaluation of this gift. For him, speaking in tongues was a beautiful gift from God, but it had to be used to build up the Church. "If I speak with human tongues and angelic as well, but do not have love, I am a noisy gong, a clanging cymbal" (1 Cor 13:1). "Thank God I speak in tongues more than any of you, but in the church I would rather say five intelligible words to instruct others than ten thousand words in a tongue" (1 Cor 14:18–19).

The gift of speaking in tongues is an integral part of the Charismatic Movement, which will be treated in the answer to the next question. Some conservative Protestants believe that the gift of tongues was only valid for the early Church, and that its current manifestation is the work of the Devil. Many other Protestants—and Catholics—believe that it is a valid gift of the Spirit.

Those who speak in tongues should not neglect spiritual guidance and sound spiritual discernment. They should ask themselves whether their gift is building up the Church and if it is bringing them closer to God.

On the other hand, those who deny the validity of this gift should ask themselves: Am I closing my mind against an authentic way of prayer? Do I believe that the Spirit can manifest Himself as He did in the early Church?

What is the Charismatic Movement?

Since the Second Vatican Council, Catholic spirituality has taken many new forms. Perhaps the largest and most influential new group has been the Charismatic Renewal Movement (sometimes called Catholic Pentecostalism). This movement began at Duquesne University in Pittsburgh in 1967. It soon spread to the University of Michigan at Ann Arbor, and to the University of Notre Dame in South Bend. Today, it influences millions of people of all ways of life, in the United States and around the world.

Pentecostal-type movements—involving a strong personal commitment to Jesus Christ, and the manifestation of the gifts of the Holy Spirit—have cropped up frequently in the history of the Church. The Montanist movement of the second century A.D., which fell into heresy, was of this type. Similar movements were common in the United States (among Protestants) in the early 19th century. Pentecostalism as such began in Topeka, Kansas in 1901. It spread rapidly and had many conflicts with more traditional Protestant Churches. The early Pentecostals felt that all other Churches were false, and that no true Christian should have anything to do with them. On the other hand, the established Churches had little sympathy for those who wanted to remain in communion with them, but still manifest the charismatic gifts.

More recently, attitudes on both sides have softened. Many traditional Pentecostals—including some of the surviving early members—now concede that the Spirit is not restricted to their own group. Charismatic forms of worship are now accepted in many Churches which formerly rejected them. The phenomenal growth of the Catholic Charismatic Movement has been a great factor in this trend towards reconciliation.

The Catholic Charismatics at the start were directly influenced by the Pentecostals. Instead of leaving the Catholic Church (which would have been the expected thing to do), they stayed in and saw that their new gifts were not foreign to Catholicism after all.

From the beginning, the leaders of this movement sought advice and support from Church authorities. The latter, for their part, have on the whole been very open to the Charismatic Movement. Paul VI and John Paul II both met with representatives of the Charismatics and gave their encouragement. Many bishops, priests and religious—the highest ranking being Cardinal Suenens of Belgium—have been actively involved. This mutual openness has kept the Catholic Charismatics from the danger of heresy or schism. It has also helped them see how their experience of the Spirit fits into the worship and devotion of the Church. One area in the beginning which called for discernment was the wholesale adoption of terms and attitudes from the traditional Pentecostals.

It came to be seen that the gifts of the Spirit, such as speaking in tongues, could be received without appropriating the rather narrow concepts common in Pentecostalism.

A great many parishes have Charismatic prayer groups which meet at regular times. The service at these meetings stresses singing, personal prayer and the reading of Scripture. The style is open and emotional. The gifts of the Spirit are manifested at these gatherings—speaking in tongues, prophecies, healings—in short, the whole range of gifts listed by Paul. A very intense conversion experience—the so-called "baptism in the Spirit"—is highly prized in Charismatic circles. Catholic Charismatics point out that this term, taken from earlier Pentecostalism, is not used in the Movement as a denial or denigration of traditional baptism. They interpret it as an unleashing of the gifts of the Spirit given to each Christian in baptism. "Slaying in the Spirit" is an experience in which the worshipper has either a momentary loss of consciousness or mobility. Those who have experienced this report that it is accompanied by a great feeling of spiritual peace, and that it has nothing to do with hysteria.

Catholic Charismatics have not downplayed the Mass. They see it and the other sacraments as vital channels of the Spirit's activity. Many report that their experiences in this movement have increased their devotion to the Mass. Charismatics have also been involved in the ecumenical movement, at the same time keeping in mind the distinctive elements of their Catholic heritage.

In 1969, the U.S. Catholic Bishops' Commission issued a report on the Charismatic Movement which is still relevant: "It must be admitted that theologically the movement has legitimate reasons for existence. It has a strong biblical basis. It would be difficult to inhibit the working of the Spirit which manifested itself so abundantly in the early Church. The participants in the Catholic Pentecostal (Charismatic) movement claim that they receive certain charismatic gifts. Admittedly, there have been abuses, but the cure is not a denial of their existence but their proper use. We still need further research on the matter of charismatic gifts."

The subject of abuses in the Charismatic Movement is an important one. The Movement is not served by ignoring possible dangers. Because it is not (and could not be) a highly centralized movement, and because it has grown very rapidly over a very short period of time, it is inevitable that problems can crop up here and there.

Some individuals and local groups have left the Catholic Church, denying the authority of the bishops and the value of the sacraments. Others, staying in the Church, look upon non-Charismatic Christians as second-rate. Others fall into an unfortunate biblical fundamentalism. Others allow themselves to be dominated by some authoritarian "charismatic" leader. These abuses are only found in a minority, and the Movement as a whole has been deeply concerned to avoid them.

The Charismatic Movement is not for everyone. The Spirit moves in many ways. Some people, because of their temperament, are uncomfortable with the emotional and uninhibited worship style fostered by the Charismatics. It is false to write them off as second-class Christians. The Church is Catholic—that is, universal. It was never intended to simply be a gathering of the elite, as the Montanists and the Novatians tried to make it.

When all is said and done, the best standard for evaluating the gifts of the Spirit and their place in the Church is found in 1 Cor 12–14. A reading of those chapters can be of great profit to all Christians, Charismatic or not.

Discussion Questions

1. How is the Spirit involved in the creation of man? Read Gn 2:7 and compare with Jn 20:22.
2. Give examples from the book of Exodus of how the Spirit worked through Moses.

3. Read and discuss Jr 31:31–34 and Ezk 36:26–27. What do these prophets tell us about the Spirit of God?
4. What are some Old Testament images used to describe the Spirit of God?
5. What does John's Gospel say about the Paraclete?
6. Give some examples of the Spirit's power from the Acts of the Apostles.
7. Read and discuss 1 Corinthians, chapters 12 to 14.
8. Using a theological dictionary, define the following terms: essence, procession, nature, substance, omnipotence, eternity, person, inspiration and generation.
9. What is the difference between the Eastern and Western positions on the procession of the Holy Spirit from the other two divine Persons?
10. Using other sources, identify these Church Fathers: Clement of Rome, Ignatius of Antioch, Tertullian, Athanasius, Basil, Gregory Nazianzen, Gregory of Nyssa, Augustine and John Damascene.
11. Research this question: What is the role of a theologian?
12. Discuss this statement: "The tradition which comes from the apostles develops in the Church with the help of the Holy Spirit. For there is a growth in the understanding of the realities and the words which have been handed down." (Second Vatican Council, *Dogmatic Constitution on Revelation*, #8)

WE BELIEVE IN MARY
THE MOTHER OF GOD

Chapter Five

WE BELIEVE IN MARY
THE MOTHER OF GOD

Mary, the Mother of Jesus, holds a unique place in the history of the Church. Since the sixteenth century, in response to the Protestant Reformation, Catholics have intensified their devotion to Mary, the Mother of God. There are litanies, living rosaries, pilgrimages, May crownings, novenas, medals, statues and special prayers in her honor. In every Catholic church there is a statue or a painting of Mary. Certainly, she has a special place in the lives of Catholics

The Second Vatican Council (1962–1965) upheld the importance of Mary. Pope John XXIII, who convoked it, said in his declaration: "We announce that the Second Vatican Council shall begin on the eleventh day of October of this year (1962). By choosing this day (the feast of the Divine Maternity of Mary), we recall to your minds that great Council of Ephesus which has such an important place in the annals of the Catholic Church."

Mary in the New Testament

The New Testament says very little about Mary. There are several reasons for this surprising feature. First, the New Testament as a whole is concerned with the person of Jesus. The Gospels describe His earthly career. Acts shows Him working in the Church. Paul writes of the meaning of Christ for the believer. The Book of Revelation shows Christ sustaining the faithful persecuted. The New Testament only deals with Mary in relation to Jesus. It stresses her fulfillment of God's plan.

As already stated, the early preaching of the Church did not concern itself with the events of Jesus' life that took place before His baptism by John. This pattern is reflected in Mark's Gospel. He mentions Mary only a few times: she comes to hear Jesus preach (Mk 3:31–35); the people of Nazareth know her well (Mk 6:3).

The infancy narratives of Matthew and Luke tell us most of what we know about Mary. The early Christian writer, Julius Africanus (*circa* 220 A.D.), in a fragment preserved in Eusebius' *Ecclesiastical History*, indicates that these traditions were handed down by Jesus' family (*E.H.* 1:7).

Matthew mentions that Jesus was virginally conceived in Mary by the Holy Spirit (Mt 1:18–25); later, the Magi came to her and Jesus (Mt 2:11); after this, Mary, Joseph and Jesus fled into Egypt to avoid Herod (Mt 2:14). Mt 12:46–50 and 13:55 are parallels, respectively, of Mk 3:31–35 and 6:3.

Luke stresses Mary's obedience to the divine will. The five Joyful Mysteries of the Rosary are taken from his account. Luke speaks of Gabriel's annunciation to Mary of the conception of Jesus by the Holy Spirit (Lk 1:26–38); of Mary's visit to Elizabeth (Lk 1:39–56); of Jesus' birth (Lk 2:1–20); of Mary's visit to the Temple (Lk 2:22–39); and of Mary and Joseph finding Jesus in the Temple discussing the Law (Lk 2:41–52). Lk 8:19–21 is a parallel of Mk 3:31–35.

Mary plays an important part in John's Gospel, although she is never mentioned by name. She starts Jesus' public career by asking Him to perform His first miracle at the wedding feast at Cana (Jn 2:4–11). She is present at the Crucifixion (Jn 19:25–27), a detail found only in this Gospel.

Acts refers to her only once. She is shown praying with the apostles after the Ascension (Ac 1:14).

Paul never mentions her by name. An indirect reference is found in Gal 4:4, "God sent forth His Son, born of a woman."

In the Book of Revelation, a mysterious woman is mentioned

who has traditionally been identified with Mary. She is clothed with the sun and has the moon under her feet (Rv 12:1); is threatened by a dragon (Rv 12:4); gives birth to a son (Rv 12:5); is hidden by God (Rv 12:6); and is pursued by the dragon (Rv 12:13–17). Modern scholars believe that the author intended this woman to stand as a symbol of God's people, from whom the Messiah came, persecuted by the Devil. Over the centuries, the Church has applied this imagery from Revelation to Mary.

The New Testament tells us nothing about Mary's birth or death; nothing about her everyday life; almost nothing about her family What it tells us is enough: Mary was the mother of the Messiah Jesus and thus, in faith, fulfilled God's will.

Mary in the Early Church

In his *Letter to the Ephesians*, Ignatius of Antioch (*circa* 107) made several important statements about Mary. He said that Jesus was "son of Mary and Son of God" (7); that "our God Jesus Christ was, according to God's dispensation, the fruit of Mary's womb, of the seed of David" (18); and that "The maidenhood of Mary and her child-bearing and also the death of the Lord were hidden from the prince of this world—three resounding mysteries wrought in the silence of God" (19).

Writing around 155, Justin Martyr, in his *Dialogue With Trypho*, stated that Mary was the new Eve, who by her obedience undid the harm caused by the disobedience of the first Eve (*Dial.* 100). A few decades later, Irenaeus made this same point, in *Against Heresies* 5:19:1. Tertullian (*circa* 210), in his work on *The Flesh Of Christ* (17), used the same imagery.

Ephraem of Syria (*circa* 370) wrote a great many poems about Mary. Besides calling her the new Eve, he stressed her sinlessness and her perpetual virginity.

In the late fourth and early fifth centuries, many of the Fathers of the Western Church, such as Jerome, Ambrose, Augustine and Peter Chrysologus wrote about Mary. By this time, devotion to her was widespread. Her title, "Mother of God," was in common usage long before the Council of Ephesus in 431. The Nestorian heresy, which touched on this, will be considered shortly.

Between 430–440, many Fathers of the Eastern Church responded to this heresy by stressing Mary's God-given privileges. To Cyril of Alexandria, she was the Mediatrix of grace; to Theodotus of Ancyra, the all-immaculate; to Proclus of Constantinople, the treasure of virginity.

John Damascene (*circa* 740) is considered the last of the Eastern Fathers of the Church. Not an especially original thinker, he summed up and systematized the teachings of his predecessors. In his work *On the Falling Asleep of the Mother of God*, he wrote: "the only begotten Son of God, being God, of the same substance of God, from this virgin and pure earth formed himself into a man." In this imagery, John called to mind Gn 2:7. Just as God formed the first Adam out of the earth, so God formed Himself into the second Adam by the "pure earth," the Virgin Mary.

The Official Teaching of the Church

Most of the heresies that cropped up in the first few centuries of Christianity questioned some aspects of the Church's teaching on the humanity and divinity of Christ. There were, however, some Marian heresies. An early sect, the Collyridians, worshipped Mary as a goddess. Cerinthus denied the Virgin Birth, saying that Jesus was the normal son of Mary and Joseph (Irenaeus, *Against Heresies* 1:26:1). A Jewish-Christian sect, the Ebionites, held similar views. Around 380, Helvidius said that Mary had had other children beside Jesus. He was answered by Jerome.

Nestorianism was first and foremost a Christological heresy. It touched on Mary because it denied the implications of her popular title, "Mother of God." Nestorius, who became the Patriarch of Constantinople in 428, taught that there were two separate persons in Jesus, one divine and the other human. Furthermore, he claimed that Mary was the mother of the human person only, but not of the divine. He denied to Mary the title "Mother of God" (Theotokos). He was condemned by the General Council of Ephesus in 431. Cyril of Alexandria's *Second Letter to Nestorius*, read before the Council and solemnly approved, said: "For it was not in the first place an ordinary man who was born of the Blessed Virgin into whom the Word of God thereafter descended, but he issued united from the very womb and therefore we say that he was born according to the flesh since he made the birth of his flesh into his own birth . . ." The Council used the Greek word "tokos" which has a wider meaning than "bearer." It includes the whole process of motherhood—conception, gestation and birth.

Cyril of Alexandria became Nestorius' most vigorous opponent. In his *Fourth Letter to Nestorius*, he said: ". . . if anyone does not confess that Emmanuel [Jesus Christ] is in truth God, and that the holy Virgin is, in consequence, Theotokos [Mother of God], since she brought forth according to the flesh the Word of God who has become flesh, let him be condemned." This statement, and others similar to it, were incorporated into the official proclamation, not of the Council of Ephesus, but of the Second Council of Constantinople (553), which also condemned the Nestorians. The Council of Ephesus preserved the tradition of the early Church and made it official. To deny it is to deny a major belief of the Church.

Succeeding Councils had to defend other aspects of Mary's role in the Church. For example, the regional First Lateran Council (649) condemned the Monothelites, who claimed that Jesus had a divine will, but not a human will. By so doing, it condemned anyone who held that Mary was not really and truly the Mother of God (Canon 3).

The General Council of Trent (1545–1563) defended Mary's

role in humanity's redemption. However, its work was not primarily to defend Mary. There are only two explicit references to Mary in its numerous decrees and canons. It emphasized Mary's sinlessness (session 4) and her exemption from Original Sin (session 5).

Finally, the Second Vatican Council (1962–1965), in the *Dogmatic Constitution on the Church* (ch. 8), devotes an entire chapter to the role of Mary in the Church. It emphasized her role as the Mother of God and the Mother of the Church. This chapter, especially, is well worth studying as a summation of the Church's teaching on Mary.

These Conciliar statements are articles of belief for all Catholics. They have preserved and developed the teaching of the early Fathers, and to deny them would be to fall into heresy. General Councils reflect the belief of the Church as a whole.

There are also many Papal statements on Mary. Although not all of these are of equal importance (some are expressions of private opinion), they should be taken seriously. They also reflect the thinking of the Church.

Here, in chronological order, are several Papal statements about the Virgin Mary:

1. Pope Siricius (392) in his letter to Anysius, Bishop of Thessalonica, spoke about Mary's perpetual virginity.
2. Pope Leo I (449), in his letter to the Emperor Flavian, re-emphasized the virginity of Mary and the Virgin Birth.
3. Pope Gregory the Great (604), in his homilies on the Gospels, stated that Mary, the Virgin Mother of Jesus, is the Mother of the Church.
4. Pope Sixtus IV (1476), in his constitution on the Church, spoke about the wondrous conception of the Immaculate Virgin Mary. We see here the idea of the dogma of the Immaculate Conception, which would be proclaimed by Pope Pius IX in 1854.
5. Pope Alexander VII (1661), in his document *On the Consul-*

tation of All, mentioned that Mary was conceived without the stain of Original Sin.

6. Pope Leo XIII (1891) in his encyclical, *The Month of October*, said that the human race has access to Jesus through Mary.
7. Pope Pius X (1904) in his encyclical, *On this Day*, stated that Mary is the Mediatrix of all graces.
8. Pope Benedict XV (1918) in an apostolic letter, expressed vividly the idea of Mary as Co-Redemptrix.
9. In his posthumous book *Journal of a Soul*, many of Pope John XXIII's devotional writings on Mary were published. These, of course, are private writings, not public doctrinal statements. They do, however, express this Pope's high regard for Mary.
10. Pope Paul VI, in his encyclical, *His Church*, stressed the importance of Mary in the history of salvation.
11. Pope John Paul II has shown his devotion to Mary by his pilgrimages, between 1980 and 1982, to the Marian shrines at Fatima in Portugal, Czestochowa in Poland, Lourdes in France, and Knock in Ireland.

All of these Conciliar and Papal statements reflect the Church's great devotion to Mary as the Mother of God. She is very much a part of the Catholic tradition.

The Marian Dogmas: The Immaculate Conception and Assumption of Mary

The dogma of the Immaculate Conception of Mary was proclaimed by Pope Pius IX on December 8, 1854. This states that Mary was free from Original Sin from the very moment of her conception. It does not mean that she was conceived miraculously, or that she was exempt from sickness, suffering or death. It is not to be confused (as often happens) with the Virginal Birth of Jesus.

At issue is the privileged position of Mary and the meaning of Original Sin. Although there are many Catholic theologies of Original Sin, they all agree that there is no salvation outside of Christ's grace, and that no one can obtain salvation by human means alone.

Until the individual is touched—in the baptism of water or of desire—by the love of God in Christ, the infinite gap between creature and Creator is not bridged. In an analogous sense, the person is in a state of sin, rebellion against God, even before any actual sins have been committed. Mary was never in this state of rebellion because of Christ's special favor in light of His coming Incarnation. In this gift of the Father, bestowed through the Son and the Spirit, Mary was saved in the most dramatic way possible. The dogma of the Immaculate Conception illustrates the uniqueness of Mary in God's salvation plan for humanity. She alone remained completely faithful to God. The state of grace given her from the first moment of her conception was preserved throughout her life. She was free from actual as well as original sin. She stands as a perpetual sign of God's special love for humanity.

The dogma of the Assumption of Mary was proclaimed by Pope Pius XII on November 1, 1950. It affirms that, at the end of her earthly life, Mary was assumed body and soul into heaven. It does not say whether she died or not, and does not say anything about the manner and time of her Assumption. As in the case of the Immaculate Conception, there are aspects of this dogma open to further theological reflection. The dogma makes it clear that Mary, the model for all believers, was assumed into heaven in a "preview" of the general resurrection.

These two dogmatic statements are formulated in very few words. They are not exhaustive. As time passes, and under the guidance of the Holy Spirit, the Church will deepen and clarify its understanding of them. Both dogmas are ultimately based on the Church's divinely guided understanding of the implications of Christ's redemption.

What about the binding force of these dogmas? Several points can be made:

1. All Catholics are bound to accept them. They are part of the Faith.
2. These two dogmas need to be interpreted in light of the centrality of Christ and also in relation to the doctrine of salvation. Most other Christian denominations do not accept these dogmas; as such, they are not as essential to the Christian message as, for example, the dogmas of the Trinity and the Incarnation are.
3. If any Catholic rejected these two Marian dogmas out of ignorance or confusion, he or she would not be considered as being outside of the Catholic community.
4. However, if any Catholic deliberately and consciously rejected these dogmas, he or she would be considered as being so outside.

Comment

Mary, the Mother of God, is a key person in the Incarnation and in the redemptive process of God's salvation. Although the Marian passages in the New Testament are few, they are of great importance. Mary is seen as a woman of faith. She believes and trusts the Word of God. From the magnificent moment of Jesus' birth from her womb, through her presence in His life, to the tragic day of His death, Mary remained loyal to God's plan. After Jesus' death, we see her present with His followers. In the following centuries, Church writers discussed and clarified her unique role in God's plan. In both East and West, Mary is admired and loved.

Eastern and Western theologians alike have expressed their insights about the Virgin Mary. Despite the schism between the two branches of the Church in the 11th century, both have remained loyal to the traditions about Mary. Both give her the highest honors due any created being. Her fame has spread throughout the world. Marian shrines have been erected at Einseidel, Switzerland; Montserrat, Spain; Pompeii, Italy; Lourdes, France; Three Rivers, Canada; Washington, D.C. and elsewhere. Devotions are directed to Mary with an abundance of medals and pictures. Many girls are named after her. The Church has put many countries, including the United States, under her protection. Millions of Catholics are led to a closer relationship with Christ by devotion to Mary. All sound Marian devotion is meant to lead the believer to Jesus.

The Second Vatican Council, in the *Dogmatic Constitution on the Church*, recognized Mary's maternal relation to the Church which flows from her divine motherhood. She is the mother of a pilgrim people, moving in their faith toward God. Consequently, this Council gave her a new title: Mother of the Church.

Special Questions

What do Protestants think about the Virgin Mary?

Protestantism is the form of Christianity which sprung up in the sixteenth century to purge the Church of perversions, abuses and excesses. Besides their protest against what Catholics now acknowledge as gross abuses, they also dissented from the Catholic Church on important points of doctrine. The principal Protestant denominations are the Methodists, Episcopalians, Baptists, Congregationalists, Lutherans, Presbyterians, Fundamentalists, and Pentecostalists. Although differences in belief exist among them, they nevertheless all agree on these points:

1. Faith in the Trinity, the Hypostatic Union, and the Incarnation, Death and Resurrection of Jesus.
2. The Bible as the primary source of religious truth.
3. Direct fellowship between God and the believer and, therefore, no need for intermediaries such as Mary and the saints. Protestants reject, in general, the status that Roman Catholics have given to Mary—as an intermediary with God.

The Protestant reformers felt that Catholics had given too much honor and glory to Mary—that they had made her almost a goddess. Luther said that he respected Mary, but that no one could ever ask her for anything. Calvin and Zwingli rejected the view that Mary was unlike the rest of the human race. They all agreed that she was the Mother of Jesus. Some rejected the notion that she was the Mother of God. The Protestant reformers stressed that Jesus, not Mary, is the intermediary between God and man.

Since there are many Protestant denominations, it is difficult to give a clear-cut answer to this question. While in total agreement about Jesus as the center of their faith, they differ on many other issues. For example, in a Presbyterian church, one would not find any pictures or statues of Mary. Yet, some Episcopalians not only erect Marian statues but entire chapels. The Episcopalians embrace a wide variety of beliefs and practices. Some are quite similar to the Methodists, some are like Roman Catholics, and many are in between. Not one of the 700 Lutheran hymns is directed to the Virgin Mary. They retain the Magnificat, but of course this Gospel prayer (Lk 1:46–55) is directed to God, not Mary. In general, Protestants do not carry the rosary, wear miraculous medals, sing Marian hymns or build Marian shrines. Most feel that Catholics have exaggerated the importance of Mary, and, therefore, have diminished the importance of Jesus.

There have been times when some Catholics have exaggerated Mary's role in salvation and have de-emphasized the effectiveness of Jesus' redemptive work. On the other hand, some Protestants have been obsessed with negative criticisms about Mary and have failed to acknowledge her unique role. Catholics and Protestants are agreed that salvation comes through Jesus Christ. Possibly, both groups may come closer as the Christological implications of the Marian dogmas become more apparent. Theologians from both groups are working to bridge these differences in faith. After all, Mary, the Virgin Mother of Jesus, belongs to all Christians as part of our common heritage.

What about private revelations by the Virgin Mary?

Private revelations are given to an individual and not to the Church. They do not demand acceptance by the faithful but, in the best of cases, inspire the faithful to live more fully the Gospel. The tradition of the Church has held that private revelations are possible and many inspirations valid. Yet, private revelations and inspirations must be treated critically because of the human elements that inevitably accompany them. They seem to be restricted to certain places, times and groups in the Church. Throughout the years and around the world, there have been claims of apparitions of the Blessed Virgin. The vast majority of these apparitions have proven to be fraudulent or due to hysteria. A few have proven themselves to have lasting inspirational impact and have enriched the faith life of countless believers. The content of the "revelations" of Fatima, Lourdes, Guadalupe, etc. is always fascinating. Nevertheless, the messages are not in any way considered to be an essential part of Catholic teaching unless the message refers to a dogma defined by the Church or contained in Scripture. Even when a particular apparition (or devotion based on an apparition) is approved by the Church, no obligation exists on the part of any Catholic to believe that an apparition took place or a revelation was given. The Church, for example, has on its liturgical calendar a feast devoted to Our Lady of Lourdes. It recognizes that the "revelation" at Lourdes contains nothing contrary to the faith. But no Catholic is bound in conscience to believe that an apparition appeared or a revelation was given at Lourdes. This is the case regardless of the historical evidence for such an event, or the spiritual and devotional benefits from such a belief.

Discussion Questions

1. Compare the accounts of Jesus' birth in Matthew and Luke.
2. Read and discuss the images of chapter 12 of the Book of Revelation as images of Mary.

3. Class project: Use theological sources to discuss the Eastern and Western Churches. How do they differ? How are they alike?

4. Use theological sources to identify the following Church Fathers: Ambrose, Jerome, Augustine, Cyril of Alexandria, Tertullian, John Damascene, and Justin Martyr.

5. What was the Nestorian heresy? How did the Church respond?

6. What is the significance of the word, Theotokos?

7. Why is the Council of Ephesus important for Mariology today?

8. Discuss the differences between Council statements and Papal documents.

9. What is meant by Original Sin?

10. Explain the Marian dogmas.

11. Rejecting a dogma of the Church means that one is outside the Catholic community. Explain.

12. Discuss the Catholic and Protestant views of Mary.

WE BELIEVE IN THE RESURRECTION

THE NEW TESTAMENT ON THE
RESURRECTION OF JESUS

THE OFFICIAL TEACHING OF THE CHURCH

THE TESTIMONY OF THE BIBLE ON THE
RESURRECTION OF THE BODY

THE OFFICIAL TEACHING OF THE CHURCH

COMMENT

SPECIAL QUESTIONS

MUST WE BELIEVE IN THE SHROUD OF TURIN?

WHAT WILL LIFE AFTER DEATH BE LIKE?

DISCUSSION QUESTIONS

Chapter Six

WE BELIEVE IN THE RESURRECTION

Jesus rose bodily from the dead. This is the central doctrine of Christianity. As St. Paul wrote to the Corinthians (1 Cor 15:14), "If Christ has not been raised, then our preaching is in vain and your faith is in vain."

From the earliest days of Christianity to our own, there have been skeptics who deny the Resurrection of Jesus. Some have said that it was a spiritual, not a physical, resurrection. Others have claimed it was a hoax. In the 1960's, Dr. Hugh Schonfield wrote a best-seller, *The Passover Plot.* He argued that Jesus arranged things so as to survive the Crucifixion (in the belief that this was to fulfill the Messianic prophecies), but that He failed and died in the tomb. His body was removed by somebody other than the apostles. Thus, Jesus' closest followers were the victims of deception, and this explains their sincerity of belief. Similar theories have been proposed in the past. None of them has held up under close scrutiny. They are based more on conjecture and creative imagination than on any hard evidence.

The believer accepts the Resurrection as it is revealed in the New Testament. Nevertheless, there are many legitimate questions. What is the origin of this belief? How did the apostles experience the Resurrection? Did Jesus have the same body after rising from the dead? How did He look after the Resurrection? What about the empty tomb? These questions and others have perplexed and stimulated theologians. They are asked, not in any distrusting manner, but to deepen our understanding of this central mystery of faith.

The study of Jesus' Resurrection is necessary, since that event is the cornerstone of Christianity. The Christian faith in the resurrection of each person is linked with Jesus' own Resurrection.

After examining the biblical and historical material relating to Jesus' Resurrection, the general resurrection of the dead will be considered.

The New Testament on the Resurrection of Jesus

The New Testament never says that anyone witnessed Jesus' Resurrection. Belief in it is based on the empty tomb and on Jesus' post-Resurrection appearances.

These appearances took place in two areas: Galilee and Jerusalem. The Gospel accounts are based on a number of earlier traditions, and thus cannot be completely harmonized with each other. It is impossible to say where the risen Jesus appeared first. Although some incidental discrepancies may exist between the different accounts, one must consider that they were written at different times and places. Sometimes, an evangelist incorporated into his account material that was not available to others. Or, at times, an evangelist gave a new slant or twist to material that they all shared. Furthermore, they wrote for different audiences and would have mentioned details that their particular audiences would have been interested in.

Jesus' appearance in Galilee is mentioned in Matthew 28 and John 21. Near His tomb, outside Jerusalem, Jesus appeared to Mary Magdalene (Mt 28:1–10; Jn 20:1–18). Luke and John place Jesus' first appearance to the apostles in Jerusalem (Lk 24:36–53; Jn 20:19–29). Luke mentions that Jesus appeared to two of His followers as they were walking to Emmaus, about seven miles from Jerusalem (Lk 24:13–35). The account of Jesus' appearances in Mk 16:9–20 (which the Church accepts as inspired) was not originally part of that Gospel. It was written later and is in fact a summary of traditions from Luke and John.

The Gospel accounts have these points in common: 1) The empty tomb was discovered by women; 2) an angel (or angels) announced the Resurrection to them; 3) the women told the apostles about this; 4) Jesus appeared to the apostles later.

However, there are different points among these writers. Matthew alone reports that guards were at the tomb and that they were bribed by the temple officials to say that Jesus' body was stolen. Luke fails to mention that Jesus appeared to Mary Magdalene, something the other three Gospels mention.

For John, the Resurrection is the sign (miracle) of Jesus' power to lay down His life and to take it up again (Jn 2:19-22; 10:17–18). It is the greatest sign which Jesus performed to show that He is the Son of God. Peculiar to John are these points: 1) Peter and the beloved disciple came to the empty tomb (20:2–10); 2) Jesus appeared to Thomas and showed him His hands and His side (20:24–29); 3) Jesus appeared to the disciples as they were fishing on the Sea of Galilee, and He commissioned Peter to "feed my sheep" (21:1–23). Many similarities exist between the accounts in Luke and John. Compare, for instance, Lk 24:36-40 and Jn 20:19–20. The risen Jesus can appear and disappear, and materialize through locked doors. Yet He can eat and be touched, and has flesh and bones. He cannot be recognized unless He wills it.

In the Acts of the Apostles, there are several references to the Resurrection. The main purpose of these accounts is to verify that the apostles are witnesses to the risen Lord. The Resurrection is a standard part of the apostle's preaching. It is seen as God's ultimate vindication of Jesus' ministry (Ac 2:22–36; 10:40–41). To an uncomprehending pagan, the subject of Paul's preaching was "a certain Jesus who had died but who Paul claimed is alive" (Ac 25:19). The risen Jesus appeared to Paul on the road to Damascus (Ac 9:1–9), but He appears as a blinding light rather than in human form.

The references to the Resurrection in the writings of Paul are very important, since these are the oldest part of the New

Testament. Paul's own encounter with the risen Jesus is mentioned in his letter to the Galatians (1:11–17). Paul's account of the other apparitions differs somewhat from that in the Gospels. Jesus was seen by Peter, then by the Twelve, then by 500 people at once, then by James, by all the apostles, and then by Paul himself (1 Cor 15:5–8). Christ risen from the dead sits at the right hand of the Father as intercessor (Rm 8:34); God has raised Jesus and exalted Him above all creatures (Ep 1:20); Jesus is the first-born of those who rise (Col 1:18); He is Lord because of the Resurrection (Ph 2:9–11). Paul saw Jesus' Resurrection as something shared in by the believer. This did not make him ignore the unique circumstances of Jesus' rising from the dead. He verified in writing the earliest tradition about Jesus' appearances after His Resurrection.

The New Testament tells us this about Jesus' appearances: 1) They were unexpected and startling; 2) Jesus appeared only to those He wished to; 3) He showed them that He was not a ghost, but was risen to a transcendent new life; 4) Those who saw Him were completely convinced; 5) Jesus commissioned them to preach and make disciples.

What About the Empty Tomb?

The Gospel accounts (Mk 16; Mt 28; Lk 24; Jn 20) contain many discrepancies. The empty tomb, strictly speaking, cannot be used as a proof of the Resurrection. We are simply told that the tomb was empty, but not how it happened. The evangelists themselves alluded to some stories that were circulating at the time about how the tomb became empty. Some people said that the disciples had stolen the body (Mt 27:62–66; 28:11–15); or (like Mary Magdalene's first reaction) believed that the gardener had taken His body away (Jn 20:13-15). The empty tomb is not a decisive proof of Jesus' Resurrection. The fact that the tomb was empty gives a basis for seeing a continuity between the pre- and post-Resurrection body of Jesus. However, it is the appearances of Jesus after His Resurrection that are most important. The apostles and others had a real experience of Jesus being alive. He spoke with them and ate with them. They touched Him and had their faith enlivened by that contact. To them, the Resurrection was the most overwhelming of experiences. It changed their lives and the life of all mankind. The New Testament shows that the Resurrection has been part of the belief of the Church from the beginning. All the Creeds mention it; all the Church Fathers upheld it; the official Church has always taught and defended it; the faithful have always believed it.

Even in Paul's time, some people denied the Resurrection (1 Cor 15:12) or interpreted it in a "spiritual," non-literal way (2 Tm 2:18). Those heretics who denied the Incarnation—such as the Docetists and the Manichaeans—obviously denied the Resurrection as well. Some heretics believed in the Resurrection without holding that this implied Jesus was equal to God. The Ebionites and the Arians are examples of this second group.

Some of the Church's official statements on the Resurrection of Jesus being a matter of belief for all Christians are contained in the following: the Apostles' Creed; the Profession of Faith of the Council of Nicaea (325); the Nicaeo-Constantinopolitan Creed (381); the Athanasian Creed (400's); the Creed of Epiphanius (374); the Formula of the "Faith of Damasus" (500's); the Formula of the "Merciful Trinity" (500's); the Lateran Council Creed (649); the Creed of the Eleventh Council of Toledo (675); the Profession of Faith of the Fourth Lateran General Council (1215); the Profession of Faith of Michael Paleologue (the Second Council of Lyons) (1274); the Creed of Pius IV (1564); and the Letter of Pius X Against the Modernists (1905).

On the Resurrection of Jesus' body specifically: the letter of Pope Leo IX (1053) to the Bishop of Antioch; the letter of Pope Innocent III (1208) to the Archbishop of Terraco; the Fourth Lateran Council (1215); and the Council of Florence (1438–1445). On the point that Jesus rose from the dead on His own power, the Eleventh Council of Toledo (675).

No truth of the Christian Faith is taught so clearly by the Fathers and Councils as is the Resurrection. The Resurrection of Jesus remains truly the keystone of the Christian Faith. Without it, as Paul wrote to the Corinthians, there is no faith.

The Testimony of the Bible on the Resurrection of the Body

Having discussed Jesus' Resurrection, our attention is focused on whether or not there will be a general resurrection of the dead.

It took many centuries for the Jews' beliefs about immortality and the resurrection of the body to develop and mature. This development can be traced in the books of the Old Testament.

At first, the ancient Hebrews had only a very vague idea of what happened after death. They held that the dead, good and bad alike, went to Sheol, a dark, gloomy underworld where they led a shadowy existence. This belief, as reflected in such passages as Is 14:9–11, is paralleled in Sumerian mythology and in Homer's *Odyssey*.

The earliest notions of resurrection involved the restoration of Israel as a nation. Hosea says that if they return to Yahweh, He will revive them after two days and on the third day will raise them up to live in His presence (Ho 6:1–2). Ezekiel symbolically portrays the restoration of Israel from the Exile as a resurrection from the dead (Ezk 37:1–14). These prophets were speaking of a political restoration, not a literal raising from the dead.

When, eventually, the Jews thought more deeply on the nature of the afterlife, they naturally saw it as a resurrection. They did not make the distinction between body and soul so natural to us. They saw man as a unit: any true life had to involve the body. The earliest explicit reference to a personal resurrection is in Dn 12:2–3, "Many of those who sleep in the dust of the earth shall awake . . ." The idea is clearly presented in the Second Book of Maccabees (2 M 7:9, 11, 23; 14:46). The Jews martyred under Antiochus IV Epiphanes looked forward to their own resurrection.

Under the influence of Greek thought, the Jews also began to accept the idea of the immortality of the soul—for example, in Ws 4:7–5:16.

In the time of Jesus, there were several different beliefs on this subject. The Sadducees, a wealthy and conservative elite, did not believe in the resurrection or in immortality (Mt 22:23 and parallels; Ac 23:8). The Pharisees, a larger and more popular group, did believe in these. In this regard, Jesus agreed with the Pharisees (cf. Mk 12:18–27). See also Lk 16:19–31, the story of Lazarus and the rich man.

As a sign of the Kingdom, Jesus raised some people from the dead: the daughter of Jairus (Mk 5:21–42 and parallels); the son of the widow of Naim (Lk 7:11–17); Lazarus (Jn 11:1–44). These do not (except the story of Lazarus) deal with the question of the general resurrection. In the Old Testament, some similar resurrections are mentioned (1 K 17:17–24; 2 K 4:18–37; 13:21).

In John's Gospel, Jesus mentions the general resurrection of the dead several times (Jn 5:21, 25, 28–29; 6:39, 44, 54). His raising of Lazarus is meant as a sign of Jesus' power to give life. He told Martha that Lazarus would rise again. She replied that she knew he would—on the last day. Jesus told her: "I am the resurrection and the life: he who believes in me, though he die, yet shall he live; and whoever lives and believes in me shall never die" (Jn 11:25–26).

These resurrections were only the foretaste of what was to come. Lazarus and the others resumed their normal lives, and they died again when their time came. The Christian hope of resurrection is bound up with the Resurrection of Jesus.

This theme runs throughout Paul's letters. It is at the heart of his proclamation of the Good News. "If the Spirit of him who raised Jesus from the dead dwells in you, he who raised Christ Jesus from the dead will give life to your mortal bodies also through his Spirit which dwells in you" (Rm 8:11). "He will give a new form to this lowly body of ours and remake it according to the pattern of his glorified body, by his power to subject everything to himself" (Ph 3:21). Many other references to resurrection are found both in Paul's letters and in his speeches given in the Acts of the Apostles.

The Book of Revelation mentions both a resurrection of martyrs who will reign on earth with Christ for a thousand years (Rv 20:4–6) and a later general resurrection (Rv 20:11–15). It is the understanding of the Catholic Church that this is not to be taken literally. Some people in the early Church—and some fundamentalists today—fell into this error. Revelation is full of symbols, and it is difficult to understand without a good, up-to-date commentary on it. It is enough here to say that the Book proclaims the triumph of Christ and His Church, and the truth of the resurrection of the dead. It cannot be understood as a book of predictions about the future and the end of the world.

We have seen how the Jews gradually came to a clearer understanding of the resurrection of the dead. For Christians, the ultimate understanding of this is found in the Resurrection of Jesus. In the Gospel accounts of His Resurrection, we get hints of what our resurrection will be like. Jesus was not an insubstantial ghost. Yet His body was glorified—He could appear and disappear at will, etc. Yet these are just hints. Many questions on this subject cannot be answered in this life. "Eye has not seen, ear has not heard, nor has it so much as dawned on man what God has prepared for those who love him" (1 Cor 2:9).

The Official Teaching of the Church

In many Creeds, Conciliar statements and Papal encyclicals, the Church has safeguarded the truth of the resurrection of the dead, recorded in Scripture. Here are some of them: The Apostles' Creed: "We believe . . . in the resurrection of the flesh"; the

Creed of Epiphanius (374): "we condemn also those who do not confess the resurrection of the flesh"; the Nicaeo-Constantinopolitan Creed (381): "We look for the resurrection of the dead, and the life of the world to come"; the Athanasian Creed (5th century): "when He comes, all men will rise again with their bodies"; the Eleventh Council of Toledo (675): "We confess that, after the example of our Head, there will be a true resurrection of the body of all the dead"; the Fourth Lateran Council (1215): "[they] will all arise with their own bodies which they have now"; Pope Benedict XII's letter "Benedictus Deus" (1336): "at the day of judgment all men will appear with their bodies"; finally, the Second Vatican Council (1962–1965) in its *Pastoral Constitution on the Church in the Modern World*: ". . . we do not know the time for the consummation of the earth and of humanity . . . but we are taught that God is preparing a new dwelling place and a new earth where justice will abide . . ." (#39).

Although the early Church clearly taught the resurrection of the dead, it did not provide any detailed explanation. Such words as "flesh" and "body" are used to present the idea, but it is understood that in the resurrection the body will be glorified as Jesus' was. However, in some sense this body will be the same as the one we have now. This has been the official teaching of the Church from the beginning.

Comment

The Resurrection of Jesus is the keystone of the faith of the primitive Church. The New Testament authors captured for us in writing the faith experiences of the Christian community. Paul says explicitly that he hands on what he himself has received (1 Cor 15:3). By the time he wrote this (*circa* 56 A.D.), the Resurrection story had already been put in creedal statements, such as "Christ died and was buried and rose from the dead," "he appeared to Peter and then to the twelve," and so forth.

In the New Testament, the Resurrection of Jesus is seen as His elevation, glorification and return to the Father. It is God's ultimate confirmation of Jesus' mission. The apostles first learned of the empty tomb, and soon after, Jesus appeared to them in a glorified state. He was not a ghost or a spiritual presence. By His Resurrection, Jesus fulfilled the Messianic hopes of the Jews and effected a great change in His disciples. No longer afraid, they were ready to preach the Good News to the world.

The Resurrection made possible a deeper presence of Jesus, through the Spirit, in His followers. His disciples now saw His earthly life in the light of the Resurrection, and this is the approach that was taken in the writing of the Gospels. Finally, His Resurrection is joined with the resurrection to life of His people. "For if we believe that Jesus died and rose, God will bring forth with him from the dead those also who have fallen asleep believing in him" (1 Th 4:14).

The Resurrection affirms for Christians the survival of the whole human being, that is, both body and soul. It verifies once and for all our hopes and dreams of everlasting life. Throughout history, people have hoped and planned for another life. Certainly God, in His loving plan for humanity, puts His stamp of approval on survival by the Resurrection of His Son, Jesus. God the Father answered our doubts with His Son's Resurrection. With this assurance, we await our own resurrection.

Special Questions

Must we believe in the Shroud of Turin?
Before we answer the question, let us examine the significance of the Shroud of Turin. Some people regard it as the burial sheet of Jesus. It is a length of ancient linen cloth housed in the Cathedral in Turin, Italy: 14 feet, 2 inches long and 3 feet, 7 inches wide. The image of a man is imprinted on the sheet. Many believe that this image is of Jesus' body.

The Shroud of Turin came into the possession of the House of Savoy in 1453 and was damaged by a fire in 1532 before being moved to Turin in 1578. Unfortunately, the shroud has an obscure history before 1354. Some writers of the 5th and 6th centuries refer to an image of Jesus which may be the Shroud. In Byzantine art in the 6th century, Jesus is sometimes portrayed in a shroud. William of Tyre, who accompanied the King of Jerusalem to Constantinople in 1171, mentioned that the Shroud of Jesus was preserved in the imperial palace. When Constantinople fell to the Turks in the 15th century, the Shroud disappeared. It then appeared in the hands of the House of Savoy. Today, it is in Turin.

What about scriptural proof that the shroud of Jesus existed? The Gospel accounts describe the burial preparation of Jesus' body. He was wrapped in a linen shroud (Mt 27:59; Mk 15:46; Lk 23:53; Jn 19:40). Before this, His body was covered with myrrh, aloes and scented oil (Jn 19:39–40). Some people believe that these may have helped create the image. Others speculate that the image was "burned" on the shroud at the moment of the Resurrection. Peter found the empty shroud in the tomb (Jn 20:6–7). Although the authenticity of the Shroud is not universally accepted by scholars, its acceptance today is gaining momentum. The rapid progress of science and scholarship have helped to increase the likelihood of its authenticity. Yet, the official Church has not defined it as a matter of Faith. It will not do so. Can one personally believe that the Shroud is the burial sheet of Jesus? Yes. Is it essential to the Catholic Faith? No.

What will life after death be like?

Many people ask this difficult question. Children will ask: can they ride their bicycles? eat ice cream? play with their dog or cat? Older people ask if their first or second husband or wife will be reunited with them. Will they be able to look like 25 if they die when they are 80? What will people do in Heaven? The questions go on and on.

Some general observations on life after death: 1) Heaven is a state of being, not a place. 2) We will ultimately possess our bodies in some way. It will be glorified, better in every way than the condition of our bodies now. 3) We cannot judge conditions in the next world by those that we know here. They cannot be the same. 4) We are happy when our lives are filled with action, fulfillment and companionship. It is reasonable to presume that this will also be the case in the life of the resurrection. 5) We know that there will be no need for the physical reproduction of our species in the resurrected state. Beyond that, we know nothing about what the nature and function of our sexuality will be. Certainly, there will be love transcending anything we can now imagine. 6) We will be with our loved ones. 7) There will be no fears, worries, jealousies, or hatreds.

Perhaps we are missing the most important idea in life after death—we will be in the presence of God, who is all love, kindness, gentleness and understanding. We worry about the conditions of the next life because we do not experience enough of these qualities in this life. And so, we want to be sure that all this will be provided for. At times, we get a glimpse of the beautiful life to come when we experience being in the company of an all-loving person. We forget about ourselves.

Jesus addressed this very human concern of ours: "In my Father's house there are many dwelling places . . . I am indeed going to prepare a place for you, and then I shall come back to take you with me, that where I am you also may be" (Jn 14:2–3).

Discussion Questions

1. Why are the Gospels "Confessions of faith"?
2. Discuss the post-Resurrection appearances of Jesus (Mt 28; Mk 16; Lk 24; Jn 20–21).
3. Discuss the accounts of the empty tomb (Mt 28:1–10; Mk 16:1–8; Lk 24:1–12; Jn 20:1–13).

4. What do the accounts of Jesus' post-Resurrection appearances have in common?
5. Why is the empty tomb less important than the appearances of Jesus to prove the Resurrection?
6. Discuss the Church's official statements on the Resurrection of Jesus.
7. Discuss the idea of the general resurrection in the Second Book of Maccabees (7:9, 11, 23; 14:46).
8. Discuss Paul's concept of the resurrection of the dead (1 Cor 15).
9. Use other theological sources to discuss the position of the Pharisees and Sadducees on the resurrection.
10. Discuss the idea of the double resurrection in the Book of Revelation (20).
11. Why is the Resurrection of Jesus the central doctrine of Christianity?
12. Discuss the theological implications of Jesus' Resurrection.

WE BELIEVE IN THE CHURCH

Chapter Seven

WE BELIEVE IN THE CHURCH

In recent times, many young people question the need for the Church. Some of them are disturbed by the human scandals or politics in the Church, or see it as a big business, only interested in money. With these criticisms in mind, we will examine the origins of the Church from New Testament days through the first few centuries. In order to develop a clearer picture of the Church's true objectives, we must get a sense of our roots—which in turn gives us an anchor for living in our complex world.

All Christians are joined in Jesus' plan for salvation. The organization we call the Church is the instrument for accomplishing this salvation. It is the divinely appointed way for Jesus' teachings to remain in focus. The Church is not just a building. It is people—people who gather together to worship God and listen to His Word. The Church includes the Pope, bishops, priests, religious, laymen and laywomen. It includes all those who have left this world in God's grace—the communion of the saints. Finally, the Church is more than people: Jesus is the Head of the Church, and the Spirit brings life and grace to the people who form His Body.

The Old Testament on the Jewish Community

In the Old Testament, we read that the formation of God's people (Israel) started with the call of their father, Abraham. God made a covenant with Abraham: he and his descendants will worship no other God, and He, in turn, will lead and bless them.

Moses and the prophets reminded the people of the covenant many times. Thus, in the Hebrew language the word *Qahal* means a congregation or assembly of the faithful.

The New Testament on the Christian Community and Hierarchy

The Greek word *Ekklesia* originally meant a legislative assembly of citizens. In the New Testament, it is used to describe the assembly of Christians. It forms the basis of our English word "ecclesiastic." Christians, like the Jews, gather together for their common worship. In this case, it involves following the teachings of Jesus who revealed so fully the Father's plan.

It would be only natural for Jesus to form a Church in establishing a new covenant with His followers. It would have been a continuity with the past. And so, as the Church moved into the Greek-speaking world, *Ekklesia* took on (for Christians) the same religious meaning as *Qahal*. Once they became clearly distinct from the Jews, the word *Ekklesia* (Church) was applied exclusively to the Christians.

In the Synoptic Gospels, the word "Church" appears only twice (Mt 16:18; 18:17). "And I tell you, you are Peter, and on this rock I will build my church and the powers of death shall not prevail against it" (Mt 16:18). "If he refuses to listen to them, tell it to the church and if he refuses to listen even to the church, let him be to you as a Gentile and a tax collector" (Mt 18:17). It must be remembered that the Gospels are products of the Church, and that each of them to some degree projects the concerns and beliefs of the time it was written into its account of Jesus. The heart of Jesus' message concerned the Kingdom of Heaven. He gathered a group around Himself and He clearly intended them to live according to His teachings to proclaim this Good News to others. It took time, under the guidance of the Spirit, for His followers to see that they were the new Israel, the new *Qahal* or *Ekklesia*. The Gospels present this idea of Jesus' community in many ways: under the image of a flock (Lk 12:32) shepherded by Jesus (Jn 10:1–18) whose place on earth Peter is appointed to fill (Jn 21:15f); under the image of children (Lk 18:16–17); of people invited to a banquet (Lk 14:16–24).

In John's Gospel, the community is described as a flock and Jesus as the Good Shepherd (10:1–5). Another image is that of the Vine and the branches (15:1–8). Jesus commits the flock to Peter (21:15–17). John does not use the word *Ekklesia* in his Gospel, but does use it in his third letter (3 Jn 6, 9, 10). An example: "I have written something to the church; but Diotrephes, who likes to put himself first, does not acknowledge my authority" (3 Jn 9).

In the Book of Revelation, the word *Ekklesia* appears twenty times. It refers always to particular churches. This Book warns the seven local churches in the province of Asia of persecutions and consoles them with the promise of the final victory of the Church, the Bride of the Lamb (Jesus).

The Acts of the Apostles uses the word *Ekklesia* twenty-three times. It always means the local church. This was organized with its own bishop, presbyters and deacons (cf. Ac 6:1–7; 20:17, 28). The church in Jerusalem, generally recognized as the first church, had a position of leadership (Ac 15:1–29).

The word *Ekklesia* occurs sixty-five times in Paul's letters. Most of the time, it means the local church. For example, it is often used in the greeting at the beginning of his letters (cf. 1 Cor 1:2; 2 Cor 1:1). However, Paul also uses *Ekklesia* in regard to the universal Church, especially in his letters to the Ephesians and Colossians. But references in other letters also exist (Gal 1:13; Ph 3:6). Paul employs various images for the Church: the Bride of Christ (Ep 5:25–26); Mother (Gal 4:26); Body of Christ (1 Cor 12); a building (Ep 2:20f); and a household (Ep 2:19).

In Paul's thought, all these local churches unite in a single organization, the Church. In all cases, the local churches are united under the leadership of Jesus. The Church admits new members by the rite of baptism, not circumcision. It is an organized group with apostles, bishops, prophets, deacons, elders, teachers and presbyters. Although the strict relationship between the mother church of Jerusalem and the other churches is not clear, all form a community transformed by the presence of the Spirit and celebrating the Eucharist. Even so, this celebration hardly required a uniform structure in all local churches.

We must also remember that in the New Testament every single follower of Jesus was called to holiness and heroic love. All of the sacraments are signs that support and make possible such a life. First of all there is baptism which incorporates a person into the living Body of Christ, His Church. It wipes away all sin. Then there is the sacrament of reconciliation that forgives sins committed after baptism and encourages the Christian to grow in virtue. The Eucharist nourishes the disciple of the Lord. In this "love feast," as the early Christians sometimes called it, he or she comes into personal contact with the Lord. In confirmation there is a special outpouring of the Holy Spirit upon the believer that is meant to sustain him or her for life in the pursuit of the Gospel values. In matrimony, two people become a living sign of Christ's love for His Church through their fidelity to one another, their life–long commitment, and their openness to have children and thus continuing the marvelous cycle of life. The anointing of the sick is a tangible extension of Christ's healing power. Holy orders provides priests to serve God's people.

All of the sacraments are channels of the Holy Spirit. The Spirit is, in fact, the soul of the Church. Without it, the Church would simply be a human organization.

The structure of the Church is important—without it, a vital element of stability, prudence and direction would be gone. Catholics (and many other Christians) believe that without this, the Church could not exist. Before considering the function of the Pope and the bishops, a closer look at the Spirit's work in the Church is in order.

In the broadest sense, the Church is much larger than anyone in this world can imagine. It includes all people of all times who have let God's grace enter their lives permanently. It includes the living and the dead. It is manifest in the Catholic Church, of course, but it is not limited to this one group. God's grace, imparted by the Spirit, touches non-Catholic Christians, non-Christians, even atheists. It is the highest presumption for any of us to judge how our fellow men or women stand in relation to God. In the sight of God, an honest atheist or a Hindu trying to live a good life, may be holier than a Catholic hypocrite or fanatic who mouths pieties and oppresses those under his authority. We should always be conscious of this. At the same time, Catholics believe that (despite the failings of many of its members) the Spirit is present in a special way in the Church and its sacraments, scriptures, worship and teaching authority, and that they have a duty to share these treasures with others. An older model of missionary thought held that non-Catholics (or non-Christians) were damned. This is clearly and absolutely rejected by the teaching Church.

This does not mean that our missionary zeal should fade. Jesus compared the Kingdom of God to a treasure (Mt 13:44) and a valuable pearl (Mt 13:46), things so valuable that a man would sell all he had to get his hands on them. We are privileged to share these treasures with others, always respecting their freedom of conscience and acknowledging that in ways unknown to us, God's grace may already be in them.

Although there are many different ministries and offices in the Church, all its members have been freed by Christ for liberty (Gal 5:1). They are called to be transformed from glory to glory into God's image (2 Cor 3:18). They are a royal priesthood (1 P 2:9). They are to be glorified with Christ (Ph 3:21) and will be like God, seeing God as He really is (1 Jn 3:2).

The Church is called to be the sign of God's presence in the world. It is, in fact, the original sacrament of God from which the seven sacraments derive. In charity, service, and holiness its members are called to live out the Gospel values. The Church is holy, even though it is stained, injured, warped and restricted by sin. In common with the rest of humanity, its members are sinners—the very kind of people Christ came for. In spite of the constant damage inflicted on it from the beginning by sin, the Church is ever renewed by the Holy Spirit. This Spirit works in many ways, ever leading the Church to a deeper understanding of the mysteries of Christ.

The different aspects of the Church—prophetic, charismatic, intellectual, hierarchical, etc.—are meant to complement each other. The fact that this does not always work in practice does not diminish their value.

St. Paul best explained this in his First Letter to the Corinthians, ch. 12. Here, he reminded his readers that they were all members of Christ's body, and that the different charisms and ministries that they had were meant to build up that body. They were not given as a pretext for jealousy and quarreling. As Paul points out, these different gifts complement each other; a Church with only one of them would be as unthinkable as a man who was all hand or all eye.

In the history of the Church, we can see how this has worked in practice. The Church has suffered greatly when some charisms or ministries were downplayed. If it is only a hierarchical structure, the Church can seem dull, cold, dictatorial, out of touch with normal life. Through the ages, the Spirit has raised up many people—men and women, religious and lay, Popes, bishops and priests, even children—to recall the Church to its holy and loving mission. The process works the other way. The prophet and the gadfly need the stability of the official Church. When this has been ignored—as the Montanists and the Fraticelli and many others ignored it—the result has been heresy, schism and destruction.

The Second Vatican Council stressed the need for all in the

Church to work together and complement each other's gifts. A reading of that Council's *Dogmatic Constitution on the Church* would be of great value for anyone who wants to know what the official thinking of the Church is on this topic.

Jesus imparted to His disciples a new concept of authority: "You know how among the Gentiles those who seem to exercise authority lord it over them; their great ones make their importance felt. It cannot be like that with you. Anyone among you who aspires to greatness must serve the rest; whoever wants to rank first among you must serve the needs of all" (Mk 10:42–44).

This has always been the ideal of the Church—an ideal, unfortunately, too often ignored. This touches on one of the greatest mysteries of the Church. It is at one and the same time the sinless Body of Christ and a community of sinners in need of redemption. This tension—so profound and mysterious, and often so painful—will continue until the end of the world.

In the 1530's, Cardinal Gaspar Contarini, one of the greatest figures in the Church and an adviser to Pope Paul III, wrote the following on the true meaning of Church authority: "The law of Christ is a law of freedom, and forbids a servitude so abject that the Lutherans were entirely justified in comparing it with the Babylonish captivity . . . A pope should know that those over whom he exercises this rule are free men; not according to his own pleasure must he command, or forbid, or dispense, but in obedience to the rule of reason, of God's commands, and to the law of love, referring everything to God, and doing all in consideration of the common good only." (Leopold von Ranke, *History of the Popes*, vol. 1, p. 102.)

A variety of Church ministries are mentioned in the New Testament, many of them dealing with authority. The apostles, the men chosen by Jesus, have a special place. Peter is recognized as their head. He is mentioned first in the lists of the apostles (Mt 10:2; Mk 3:17; Lk 6:14; Ac 1:13) and plays a prominent role in Acts. Paul calls him a pillar of the Church (Gal 2:9). The elders, or presbyters (from which "priest" derives) handled Church affairs (Ac 14:3). At the beginning, the distinction between them and the bishops (1 Tm 3:1–7; Tt 1:7–9; Ac 20:17, 28) is rather vague. Soon the bishop came to be seen as the main head of the community who celebrated the Eucharist, with the presbyters as his assistants. Deacons (Ac 6:1–6; Ph 1:1; 1 Tm 3:8–13) assisted in charitable works and in preaching. Prophets and teachers also had a place in the early Church structure (Ac 13:1–3).

The authority of the Church derived from Christ, but it took some time for the forms in which this authority was exercised to become stabilized. By the time of Ignatius of Antioch (107), the threefold division of bishop, priest and deacon had become the norm. Some years earlier, Clement of Rome, in his *Letter to the Corinthians*, stressed how the bishops derived their authority from the apostles, who derived it from Christ, who derived it from God (*1 Clem.* 42:1–5; 44:1–2).

The question of the authority of the Pope has caused much controversy over the centuries. It was a key factor in the schism between East and West. It was rejected by the Protestant Churches. Even though recent ecumenical discussions have brought up many areas of agreement, important differences remain. A more extensive look at this issue is now in order.

The Official Teaching of the Church on the Primacy of Rome

In the following centuries, three ideas enhanced the role of the Bishop of Rome among the churches. First, according to the New Testament, Jesus chose Peter as the head of the apostles, thereby giving him the leadership of the Church. Therefore his successors, the Bishops of Rome, inherited that leadership. Second, the figure of Peter was linked with the biblical images of shepherd, gatekeeper, preacher and martyr. Third, Rome was the capital of the Roman Empire. Its enormous prestige "rubbed off" on the Christian community there.

The image of Petrine leadership became clearer and more focused in the first few centuries of the Church.

Pope Clement of Rome (94) wrote a letter to the church in Corinth demanding the restoration of certain presbyters who had been deposed. Although the apostle John was probably still alive at this time, too much should not be made (in view of our scanty knowledge of Church affairs at this time) of this. Clement unquestionably spoke from a position of authority as Pope. It should be kept in mind that the churches of Rome and Corinth were also linked by St. Paul, and that we do not really know how closely the Johannine church in Ephesus kept in touch with the other churches.

One of Ignatius of Antioch's (107) letters was addressed to the church at Rome. That community was described as having a primacy of love over the other local churches. Ignatius stressed the importance of the local bishops, as well as the offices of presbyter and deacon.

Irenaeus of Lyons (140–202) gives the first clear evidence for Rome's apostolic succession. Of "the very great, the very ancient and universally known church founded and organized at Rome by the two most glorious apostles, Peter and Paul," he said that "it is a matter of necessity that every church should agree with this church, on account of its pre-eminent authority" (*Against Heresies* 3:3:2).

Pope Victor I (190–198) set one date for Easter for the entire Church and threatened to excommunicate anyone who would not accept it. This was a clear manifestation of the power and authority of the Bishop of Rome. This authority was not undisputed. Bishop Polycrates of Ephesus defied Victor on the basis of the apostolic tradition of his own community. Irenaeus helped to reconcile the different parties in this dispute (Eusebius, *Ecclesiastical History* 5:23–24).

Tertullian (160–220) wrote against various heresies. In his *Prescription of Heretics*, he stated that any church which held the same faith as the churches founded by the apostles is connected with the apostolic line. He went on to say that the churches in Africa founded from Rome were truly apostolic. Ironically, Tertullian himself later became a heretic (a Montanist) and rejected the authority of the Bishop of Rome.

Cyprian of Carthage (200–258) was concerned with the visible unity of the Church. He was especially concerned about this when a Roman priest named Novatian declared himself Pope in opposition to the Pope legitimately presiding at the time. Cyprian himself did not speak of the primacy of Rome in an absolute way. There are two versions of his work on *The Unity of the Catholic Church*, both considered by scholars to be authentic. One stresses the primacy of Peter very strongly; the other is less enthusiastic and may reflect quarrels Cyprian had with Pope Stephen on the subject of baptism.

Augustine (354–430) and Jerome (340–420) were concerned to be in union with the thinking of the Bishop of Rome. Yet, the universal jurisdiction of Rome over all the Church is not explicitly mentioned by either man.

The letters of Pope Leo I (440–461), Pope Gelasius (492–496) and Pope Gregory I (590–604) stated that the fullness of power in the Church rested with the Bishop of Rome.

All these Fathers witness to the historical fact that Rome, from an early period, held special place of honor among the churches.

At this point, we shall examine the Conciliar evidence for the Primacy of Rome.

1. The First General Council of Nicaea (325) said that the Bishops of Rome, Alexandria and Antioch held special status as patriarchial areas of jurisdiction. The bishops of Carthage, Ephesus, Caesarea, Heraclea and Arles were metropolitans (a less prestigious juridical position).
2. The Council of Sardi (373) proclaimed Rome's primacy over

all other bishops of the West. The Council of Rome (378) placed all metropolitan bishops under the jurisdiction of the Bishop of Rome. While these two Councils were provincial, they reflect the historical development of the Primacy of Rome.

3. The First General Council of Constantinople (381) decreed that the Bishop of Constantinople was to have precedence of honor immediately after the Bishop of Rome, to whom it continued to give first place.

4. The other General Councils of Ephesus (451), of Constantinople II (553), and of Constantinople III (680) recognized the primacy of Rome over the Western Church but not always over the Eastern Church. The jurisdictional power of Rome was limited when it came to the affairs of the Eastern Church. It had some but it was not always universally accepted.

5. The General Council of Florence (1439–1445) decreed the universal primacy of the Bishop of Rome.

6. The General Council of Trent (1545–1563) stated that the Roman Pontiff (the Pope) is the visible head of the entire Church.

7. The First General Vatican Council (1869–1870) spoke of the primacy and defined the infallibility of the Pope.

8. The Second General Vatican Council (1962–1965) spoke in pastoral terms. The Pope is the father of the family of all Christians. His authority is to be exercised as a service and in a collegial manner. This Council reaffirmed the Primacy of Rome.

The first three centuries of Christianity saw the emergence of the Faith in a practical world. Centers of Christianity sprang up in the major cities of the Roman Empire: Rome, Alexandria, Antioch, Jerusalem and Constantinople. As heresies developed during these early centuries, the heretics and orthodox alike looked to Rome for the final decision on their doctrines. Many Church writers gave Rome a special place of honor in the Church. Some recognized the Bishop of Rome as the successor of Peter, thereby recognizing the universal jurisdictional power of Rome. On several occasions, a Pope (Victor, Leo I, Gelasius, Gregory I) clearly acted in the firm belief of the Primacy of Rome. All General Councils before the fifteenth century show a gradual recognition of the universal jurisdiction of Rome over all Church matters. Although accepted in the Western part of the Church, the Eastern part did not accept it in all matters at all times. The General Councils of Florence, of Trent and Vatican I proclaimed the Primacy of Rome. The First General Vatican Council defined the infallibility of the Pope. As can be seen, the Primacy of Rome (the recognition of the Pope as the successor of Peter and head of the Universal Church) developed very slowly but nevertheless surely.

The Second Vatican Council recognized that Jesus conferred the leadership of the Church on Peter and, in turn, his successors. However, it viewed the Primacy of Rome in collegial terms. The Pope's headship does not diminish the pastoral authority of the bishops. As a body, the latter are the successors of the apostles.

In light of all of the above, what a Catholic must believe about the nature of the Church in regard to the Roman Primacy can be summarized as follows:

1. The Church was founded by the God-Man, Jesus Christ.
2. Christ founded the Church in order to continue His work of redemption for all time.
3. Christ gave His Church a hierarchical constitution.
4. The powers given to the apostles have descended to the bishops.
5. Christ appointed the apostle Peter to be the first of all the apostles, and to be the visible head of the whole Church.
6. The successors of Peter in the Primacy are the Bishops of Rome.

7. The Pope possesses full and supreme power of jurisdiction over the whole Church in matters of faith, morals, discipline and the government of the Church.
8. The Pope is infallible when he speaks ex cathedra.

The General Councils made each of these statements; therefore, they are binding on the Church. Each dogmatic statement represents the general thinking of the Catholic community and is in continuity with the Bible. Each dogma remains open to being understood in a deeper way, as humanity's intellectual development progresses, and under the guidance of the Holy Spirit. This "development of doctrine" was discussed at great length in the 19th century by John Henry Cardinal Newman, whose cause for canonization is being considered in Rome.

Comment

Jesus' preaching centered on the Kingdom of God. Guided by the Spirit, His disciples saw that Jesus Himself is the embodiment of the Kingdom. Their preaching centered on Jesus as they looked forward to the full realization of the Kingdom at the end of time. Jesus emerges as the founder of a new community, soon called the Christian Church. A community has common goals, a common life, a common vision and a common hope. And so the Greek word *Ekklesia*, like the Hebrew word *Qahal*, came to mean a people called together by God. The new Christians became a Church rather than simply a group of individuals.

Since Jesus left no formal, detailed structure, it was natural for His disciples to form one. The New Testament describes Peter's leadership in the newly formed community in very general terms. Yet he had a unique status in regard to Jesus and his fellow disciples. He emerged as the leader of the community, governing with a sense of collegiality and not as one with the power of a dictator. Many others, such as James and Paul, had considerable authority in the early Church. Peter's advice to his fellow Church leaders is still valid: "Be examples to the flock, not lording it over those assigned to you" (1 P 5:3).

In the early Church, leadership rested with bishops, presbyters (priests) and deacons. Yet the idea of the Bishop of Rome's special jurisdiction had already emerged. During these three centuries, a number of Popes vigorously claimed universal jurisdiction over the other bishops in the different communities. However, this primacy of jurisdiction was not universally recognized.

The fourth and fifth centuries were marked by the Arian, Apollinarian, Macedonian, Nestorian and Eutychian heresies. The condemnation of these heresies enhanced the importance of the Pope. Again, the local churches looked to Rome for the final decision. The political and social prestige of Rome influenced this, but this cannot compare with the spiritual prestige the Pope enjoyed as the successor of St. Peter.

In the ninth and tenth centuries, partly because of unstable political conditions, the Primacy of Rome in the West was secured not only in religious matters but in secular as well. The Eastern Church, however, became less willing to acknowledge Roman claims in any field. A schism in the ninth century did not last long, but the schism between East and West in 1054 became permanent. In the Eastern Orthodox view, the Pope, while having a place of honor as Peter's successor, is at most only first among equals in regard to his fellow bishops. They do not recognize Papal Infallibility.

In the following centuries, the Papacy reached its greatest position of power. The religious groups which opposed it, such as the Albigenses, Waldenses, Lollards and Hussites, were crushed. However, the Protestant reformers of the sixteenth century succeeded where these groups failed. Rejecting the Papal claims as a perversion of the Gospel, they came to power in large sections of northern Europe. From that time up to the Second Vatican Council (1962–1965), the Primacy of Rome was a great source of division between the Churches. To a lesser degree, it still is.

The Second Vatican Council has given a new insight into this question. Papal authority was not intended to crush out all diversity in the Church. As a sign of unity, it must also foster a legitimate diversity. In the past, because of many challenges— political, military, social and religious—the Papacy did not always respect this. It tended to foster a static authoritarianism in the Church, in which no voice had any importance save the Pope's. It forgot some of its biblical roots.

Today the Papacy faces two challenges: 1) It must not undermine the oneness of the Church; 2) it must not destroy the diversity which must exist within the Church.

The issue of the Roman Primacy, while rooted in the New Testament, must always be seen in the concrete history of the Church. The Church is coming to see it more and more as a ministry of service. Too often in the past it was considered largely in terms of power and privilege. The different Churches are divided on the question of the Papacy. Some Lutherans and Anglicans are prepared to recognize the Papacy as a ministry of unity, but they do not believe that it is an absolutely necessary feature of the Church. Serious differences of opinion between the Churches still exist on this and other points.

Special Questions

Is the Pope Infallible?
For over eighteen hundred years the Church did not have a solemn declaration of faith on Papal Infallibility. And yet, the Church survived very well because the authority of the Pope was recognized in practice. Papal Infallibility was officially defined at the First Vatican Council (1869–1870). The reasons are many, both political and spiritual. The First Vatican Council proclaimed that the infallible teaching of a Pope is the concrete expression of the faith of the whole Church. The Pope speaks infallibly when three conditions are fulfilled: 1) when he speaks to the entire

membership of the Church; 2) on matters of faith and morals; 3) as supreme head of the Church. Obviously, there are many times when he does not speak in such a manner. That seems to be the problem. Many people think that Papal Infallibility means that he is infallible whenever he speaks. He does not speak infallibly when he speaks about current events, or gives personal interviews and so forth. He, like anybody else, can be wrong in those instances or similar ones.

In the history of the Church, only two cases can be cited when Papal Infallibility was unquestionably used. These are the definition of the Immaculate Conception of Mary (issued by Pope Pius IX in 1854) and the definition of the Assumption of Mary (issued by Pope Pius XII in 1950). Again, these beliefs were held by Church members for centuries. The Popes did not invent new teachings, but gave formal expression to beliefs already held. The purpose of Papal Infallibility is to protect divinely revealed truth. Statements like the Apostles' Creed are also infallible because they have been so universally accepted by the Church that the Pope has never had to infallibly ratify them. A Catholic who denies either a creedal statement or an infallible definition is considered outside the Church.

What must Catholics believe?

This question is closely related to the prior one. However, there are some distinctions which must be made. The Church's teachings fall into four categories: 1) infallible teachings; 2) non-infallible teachings; 3) personal opinions; and 4) disciplinary rules.

Infallible teachings are basic to the Faith and must be accepted by every Catholic. These include dogmatic teachings on the divinity of Christ, the Trinity, etc. A Catholic who consciously and deliberately denies any of these teachings is considered to be outside the Church.

Non-infallible teachings must be taken very seriously, but

it is possible to dissent from these and still remain within the Church. The teaching against artificial birth control must be taken seriously, but has not been infallibly defined.

The personal opinions of Popes, bishops, theologians and official ministers of the Church can be accepted or rejected without any penalties. To indiscriminately disregard these opinions, however, would be foolish. There is often significant value in them.

The purely disciplinary rules of the Church are made for the common good of the community. Since we belong to a community, it makes sense to follow them. Yet, a Catholic could disregard some of these and remain in good standing in the Church.

When team members work together, all benefit from it. When they do not, all suffer to some degree. When the infallible statements of the Church are put into practice, when the opinions of the Church leadership are taken seriously, and the disciplinary rules of the Church enforced, the Catholic community flourishes.

Discussion Questions

1. Discuss the meaning of *Qahal* and *Ekklesia*.
2. Discuss Paul's concept of the Church.
3. Use a theological dictionary to define: bishop, presbyter, deacon, prophet, elder, apostle.
4. Discuss the statements of Clement of Rome, Ignatius of Antioch, Irenaeus of Lyons, Pope Victor I, Tertullian, Cyprian of Carthage, Augustine and Pope Leo I on the Primacy of Rome.
5. What General Councils recognized the Primacy of Rome?
6. Which General Council defined the Infallibility of the Pope?
7. Using other theological sources, discuss Protestant attitudes to Papal authority.
8. Discuss 1 Peter 5:3 on how Church authority should be exercised.
9. Class project: Using other theological sources, discuss why

Rome, Alexandria, Antioch, Jerusalem and Constantinople became centers of Christianity.

10. In your own words, why must the Primacy of Rome be seen in a biblical, social, political, and theological context?

11. What was the Second Vatican Council's insight into unity and diversity in the Church?

12. Read and discuss the Second Vatican Council's *Constitution on the Church in the Modern World*.

WE BELIEVE IN ONE BAPTISM

Chapter Eight

WE BELIEVE IN ONE BAPTISM

Baptism has been described as our birth into Christianity. It is the beginning of a new and wonderful life. It is a sign of our dedication to Christ's mission. It makes a person a sharer in God's grace. The word "baptism" came from the Greek word *baptisma*, "immersion." *Baptizein* in Greek means "to dip or immerse."

The rite of washing or bathing has long existed as a religious practice. In the ancient world, the waters of the Ganges in India, the Euphrates in Babylonia, and the Nile in Egypt were used for sacred baths. However, these baths were more ritualistic than moralistic. Ritual baths were also prescribed for the Jews. Later Judaism, especially among the Qumran sect, saw a moral dimension in these ritual baths. In Christianity, the idea of the need for moral repentance and faith in Christ was merged with the physical cleansing of the ritual bath.

The Testimony of the Old Testament

The purifying role of water is very evident in the Old Testament. Baths were prescribed for various kinds of ritual impurities: one had to bathe after being cured of leprosy (Lv 14:8–9); after contracting personal uncleanness (Lv 15:11, 13, 16); after touching a corpse (Nb 19:19); and after sexual relations (Lv 15:18). However, these were ritual purifications. There was no moral purpose to them.

This general custom of ritual washings and bathings was

extended to the proselyte baptisms prescribed for Gentile converts. This consisted of three parts: circumcision, baptism, and sacrifice.

Once these three steps were completed by the proselyte, he was incorporated into Judaism. The idea of moral repentance was connected with this ritual washing. Many Gentiles observed Jewish customs and worshipped at synagogues, but did not become proselytes. These are the "God-fearers" mentioned in Acts. There was a great deal of Jewish missionary work in the time of Jesus. Proselytes were in the crowds that heard the apostles speak on Pentecost (Ac 2:11). One of the first deacons, Nicolaus, was a proselyte (Ac 6:5). When some of these people became Christians, the idea of a ritual bath that demanded moral repentance and symbolized entrance into a new life was already familiar to them.

The first clear statement about a moral washing or bathing comes from the Dead Sea Scrolls, discovered in 1947. These are the writings of the Essenes, a Jewish sect that existed in the time of Jesus. The Essenes did not worship in the Temple of Jerusalem, and lived a monastic life by the Dead Sea. Their Manual of Discipline states that every member had to submit to a ritual moral washing (baptism) once a year at Pentecost. A member had to be truly repentant at this time before God would forgive his sins.

The Old Testament mentions ritual bathing for various impurities. The Essene moral washings performed at Qumran (16 miles from Jerusalem) are different from these. Some scholars believe that John the Baptist was influenced by the Essenes. Whether or not this is true, John and the Essenes had some ideas in common about a ritual bath as a symbol of moral renewal. There is a great difference between this and Christian baptism. Circumcision, not baptism, is the rite of entrance into Judaism. The Christian concept of a new life in the Spirit through baptism has no equivalent in these earlier rites.

The Testimony of the New Testament

The Gospels rarely mention baptism, and it is uncertain whether Jesus Himself ever performed baptisms. At the end of Matthew's Gospel, the risen Jesus is shown as commanding His disciples to baptize in the name of the Father, the Son, and the Holy Spirit (Mt 28:19). In the equivalent scene in Mark's Gospel, Jesus says, "He who believes and is baptized will be saved; but he who does not believe will be condemned" (Mk 16:16). It is the common consent of scholars that these passages reflect the faith of the early Church rather than what Jesus actually said. In the Gospels, John the Baptist is seen as Jesus' precursor. John proclaimed a baptism of repentance (Mk 1:4). He is quoted as saying that Jesus will baptize in the Holy Spirit and in fire (Lk 3:16). Luke sees this as being fulfilled in the outpouring of the Spirit on Pentecost (Ac 1:5) and in the later manifestations of the Spirit (Ac 11:16). The Gospel of John provides an interesting piece of information not recorded by the Synoptics: for a while, Jesus and His disciples conducted a baptizing ministry similar to John's (Jn 3:22–26; 4:1–3). In this Gospel, Jesus is shown as teaching that "unless one is born of water and the Spirit, he cannot enter the Kingdom of God" (Jn 3:5). This most likely reflects the sacramental teaching of John's community at the time this Gospel was written. To varying degrees, the Gospels read their contemporary concerns into their accounts of Jesus.

Acts stresses the importance of baptism in the early Church (2:38, 41; 8:12–13, 16, 37–38; 9:18; 10:47; 19:3–5). The message of the apostles was simple: "You must reform and be baptized, each one of you, in the name of Jesus Christ, that your sins may be forgiven; then you will receive the gift of the Holy Spirit" (Ac 2:38). These passages show what the early Church believed and practiced concerning baptism.

Paul also stresses the need for baptism: "Do you not know

that all of us who have been baptized into Christ Jesus were baptized into His death?" (Rm 6:3); "For by one Spirit, we were all baptized into one body—Jews or Greeks, slaves or free—and all were made to drink of one Spirit" (1 Cor 12:13); "For as many of you as were baptized into Christ have put on Christ" (Gal 3:27). For Paul, baptism is a rebirth and regeneration.

The Official Teaching of the Church

The early writings of the Church clearly show that baptism was being practiced.

The *Didache* (late 1st century or early 2nd century), an extremely early Church manual, says: "pour water on the head three times, in the name of the Father and of the Son and of the Holy Spirit" (7:2–3). Justin Martyr's *First Apology* (2nd century) shows that baptism was practiced and that it was also followed by the Eucharist (1:61).

Hippolytus' *Apostolic Tradition* (3rd century) states that the baptismal rite was in the following question and answer form. "Do you believe in God the Father Almighty?" The candidate answers: "I believe." Then he baptizes him once. The minister asks again: "Do you believe in Jesus Christ the Son of God, who was born of the Holy Spirit and the Virgin Mary, suffered under Pontius Pilate, died, and on the third day arose from the dead?" The candidate answers: "I believe," and is baptized a second time. The minister once again asks: "Do you believe in the Holy Spirit, the Holy Church and the resurrection of the body?" The candidate replies: "I believe," and is baptized the third time (20–21).

Tertullian's *On Baptism* (3rd century) mentions that an anointing, a sign of the cross, and a prayer were added to the baptismal rite (ch. 4). Ambrose's *On the Mysteries* (4th century) also refers to this (ch. 4).

The General Councils of the Church have often dealt with baptism. The General Council of Ephesus (431) condemned the baptismal ideas of Donatus, an African bishop, and Pelagius, a British layman. The Donatists claimed that those who left the Church must be rebaptized if they reentered. The Pelagians taught that there is no original sin for baptism to wash away.

The Second General Lateran Council (1139) condemned Peter de Brius (his followers were called Petrobrosians), who rejected the baptism of infants. The Third General Lateran Council (1179) did the same in regard to Constantine of Samosata, who was connected with the Albigenses.

The Fourth General Lateran Council (1215) stated that anyone can administer baptism according to the form laid down by the Church. That is to say, a priest or deacon is the usual minister of baptism, but in a case of necessity (such as danger of death) anyone (Christian or non-Christian) can baptize providing the person baptizing has the intention of doing what the Church does in baptism.

The General Council of Trent (1545–1563) condemned anyone who held that John the Baptist's baptism had the same effective power as the baptism of Christ. It also declared that water— not any fluid—was necessary for a valid baptism; that the Trinitarian formula must be said; and that baptism is necessary for salvation (what the Church means by this is discussed later in this chapter). The Council affirmed that the baptism of young children is valid, rejecting the Anabaptists' (a Protestant sect) custom of only baptizing those who reached the age of reason. Because of the Protestant Reformation, the Catholic Church had to clearly state what its constant beliefs and practices were. The Council of Trent attempted to do this.

Whether through Papal or Conciliar statements, the Church has officially upheld the idea that Christ instituted baptism. The New Testament does not tell us exactly how the baptismal rite was performed. In the Acts of the Apostles, we read of how the apostles carried out Jesus' mandate to baptize. Early Church documents such as the *Didache* show that this apostolic tradition was continued. Some rites, such as the anointing of the head, were added later to enhance the baptismal rite. One of the official Church's functions is to preserve what has been handed down and to pass it on to future generations.

Comment

As we have seen, the apostles baptized after Jesus' Resurrection. This baptism, like John the Baptist's, demanded a moral conversion. The great difference between the two is that the Holy Spirit is given in Christian baptism. Another distinction of Christian baptism is the profession of faith in Jesus. This is referred to in the Acts of the Apostles (22:16). The later baptismal profession of faith preserved by Hippolytus stressed belief in the Father, the Son and the Holy Spirit .

Paul provides various concepts and images of the meaning of being baptized into Christ. Those being baptized receive new life in Christ (Col 2:11–13); for them, the power of sin and death is broken (Rm 6:1–11). Because of Paul, the early Church had a profound theology of baptism.

During the first three centuries of the Church, the idea spread that serious sins committed after baptism could only be forgiven by an extremely long and harsh penance. It is not surprising that some people delayed their baptism until they were on their deathbeds. This was the case with the Emperor Constantine. When Christianity became legal in the fourth century, and increasing numbers of people joined the Church, it came to be seen that this view of baptism was wrong. It became clearer that sins committed after baptism could be forgiven. Many Church Fathers stressed that baptism was meant to be the beginning of one's life in Christ here and now—not just at death.

In each century, the Church had to deal with accusations against baptism. Sometimes the questions centered on the baptismal form or the proper minister of baptism. Other times, the controversy centered on the effects of baptism or on who the recipient should be. Each challenge forced the Church to consider the deeper implications of baptism.

Even in our own age, we face challenges in the area of baptism. The Second Vatican Council (1962–1965) gave new insights and restated the age-old teaching of the Church. It stressed the idea that baptism creates a sacramental bond uniting and linking all who have been reborn by means of it (*Decree on Ecumenism*, 22). It affirmed Paul's idea that baptism plunges a person into the Easter mystery of Christ (*Constitution on the Sacred Liturgy*, 6). Also, it stressed that God does not deny the help necessary for salvation to those who, without blame on their part, have not come to the explicit knowledge of God but who strive to live a good life (*Dogmatic Constitution on the Church*, 16).

Today's theologians have expressed their insights—which must be seen in the context of the Church's teaching on baptism, and subject to the teaching authority of the Church. Eugene Maly says that baptism makes a person more aware of being a community member in the Church, rather than just being an individual. Edward Schillebeeckx says that baptism of desire for unbaptized infants is sufficient for salvation although the actual reception of the sacrament of baptism remains necessary when available.

It is important to remember the fundamental point about baptism: it initiates a person into the life of Christ. Therefore, great care must be taken in this area. That is why the Second Vatican Council decreed its restoration, revision and accommodation to local traditions. All this, done in conformity with the ancient teachings of the Church, is intended to stress the key place of baptism in the Christian life.

Special Questions

Can non-Catholics be godparents for a Catholic infant or adult?

The answer to the question is, no. At first it may sound harsh and severe, ·but the reason is quite simple and logical.

First, the godparents are expected to accept the responsibility of raising the baby in the Catholic Faith. How can a non-Catholic godparent do it without being well-versed in that Faith? Second, during the ceremony the godparents are asked to make a profession of faith (similar to the one Hippolytus mentioned). Certainly the non-Christian godparent could not truthfully answer these questions in the affirmative. Third, the baptism of the child requires the godparent to make the promises for the child. Frankly, it would be hypocritical. Fourth, the law of the Catholic Church expressly prohibits such a practice. Every organization, whether it be a sports team, a store, or a hotel chain, has the right to make its own rules for the well-being of its members. These are made not only for the good of the individual, but also for the community to which he or she belongs. So, the Church has this right. The Catholic Church explicitly states that there must be at least one Catholic godparent who will be able to help the parents, if necessary, to raise the child as a practicing Catholic. This Catholic godparent must have been baptized and confirmed and received the Eucharist. Furthermore, in the case in which only one godparent is present, the Church allows the godparent to be either a man or a woman. A sponsor must normally be at least sixteen years old. He or she must have received the three sacraments already mentioned.

Four final points remain to be considered: 1) the non-Catholic who is asked to be a godparent assumes a very uncomfortable position inasmuch as they are being asked to violate their conscience; 2) a baptized non-Catholic may be asked to be an official witness for the baptism of a Catholic infant or adult (the witness' name would appear on the baptismal certificate); 3) often this problem involves extremely emotional issues because of mixed marriages, etc.; 4) most Protestant Churches will not permit their members to be a godparent for a Catholic.

What happens to unbaptized infants?

The New Testament regards baptism as necessary for salvation. What about unbaptized babies? Why punish an innocent baby for the faults of a parent or someone who neglected to have them baptized? If God is truly good and just, how can He punish this innocent baby by depriving it of Heaven? It seems unfair, grossly severe and harsh.

These questions and statements have bothered Christians since the first century. What is the solution? Let us see the problem in its historical setting.

In the fifth century, Augustine stated that unbaptized babies went to Hell. He was not comfortable with this idea, but in his understanding of grace could see no alternative. This view was not shared by some other Fathers, such as John Chrysostom. Augustine held that all people were so tainted by original sin that they could only go to Hell. Only a select group, baptized Christians who died in a state of grace, could go to Heaven. Augustine's view, much harsher than that of the official Church, has unfortunately had an immense impact on Christian thought and practice. It served as an incentive for people to have their children baptized as soon as possible, but it was an incentive of terror.

In the eleventh century, Anselm made a theological conclusion that there was a part of Hell reserved for these innocent babies (and virtuous pagans who had never heard of Christ). He called it Limbo. In the thirteenth century, the great theologian, Thomas Aquinas elaborated on this. He stated that it is a place where the souls of those who are barred from Heaven through no fault of their own enjoy a certain natural happiness.

But these are speculations. What are we to believe? The

following should be kept in mind. 1) the idea of Limbo is simply a theological theory and *not* a dogma; 2) Limbo for unbaptized infants was a sincere attempt to console the living while protecting the necessity of baptism; 3) contemporary theology offers alternative and more satisfying explanations of the possible fate of unbaptized innocents.

Though Limbo would be a pleasant enough situation, the person nevertheless would be cut off from God for eternity in a part of Hell. Yet, to say that babies automatically go to Heaven because they have not had the opportunity to commit any personal sin would be to imply that they did not need Christ for their salvation. Alfred Vanneste, a contemporary theologian, has pointed out that although the child has not committed any personal sin, neither has that child had the opportunity to do any act of kindness or personal act of love. Therefore the child can only be called "innocent" or "sinful" in an analogous sense. Vanneste speculates that at the moment of death the infant is given a special grace to personally choose to reject or accept the grace of Christ. If the infant accepts it he or she in effect receives a baptism of desire and is accepted into Christ's heavenly kingdom. Since the infant has not been tainted by the poison of actual sin up until that point, then there would be little reason to reject the offer of grace. Nevertheless, Christ "forces" no one to enter His kingdom. He invites in love and the infant too is at the moment free, according to Vanneste, to sin. Nevertheless, sustained by the love of the parents and the prayers of the universal Church, it is unlikely that the infant would slip through the grasp of the Lord of love.

Discussion Questions

1. What was a proselyte baptism in Judaism? What were its three steps?
2. From another source, briefly describe the Dead Sea Scrolls.

3. What is the difference between a Jewish ritual washing (sometimes called a baptism) and a Christian baptism?
4. What is the difference between John the Baptist's baptism and Christ's baptism?
5. Show from the Acts of the Apostles that baptism was practiced in the early Church.
6. What were the two major heresies that attacked the official Church position on baptism?
7. Why was the Council of Trent so important for the baptism issue?
8. What is the function of a General Council?
9. What did Paul contribute to the theology of baptism?
10. What did the Second Vatican Council say about baptism?
11. Discuss the justice of the Limbo question.
12. Discuss Alfred Vanneste's ideas on the salvation of unbaptized babies.

WE BELIEVE IN THE AFTERLIFE

Chapter Nine

WE BELIEVE IN THE AFTERLIFE

Death has always been a popular subject. It is universal and inevitable. Young and old talk about it. Universities have courses on death. Churches offer prayers for the dead. Ministers discuss ways to deal with death. Authors write books on death. At the root of all of this, there is the question of life after death.

Jesus spoke about death and an afterlife. For those faithful to the message of God, there is an eternal reward in Heaven. We will discuss the Jewish concept of the afterlife, and then the Christian concept. Some of this material has already been discussed from a different perspective in the chapter on the Resurrection.

The Testimony of the Old Testament

In much of the Old Testament, death is viewed as the end of all pain and sorrow. It is the final separation from this life. For the Hebrews, a long life indicated that God was pleased with a person. For example: "if your heart turns away and you will not hear, but are drawn away to worship other gods and serve them . . . you shall perish" (Dt 30:17–18). The Psalmist (Ps 55:24) says that God will bring a premature death upon the sinner.

Death, for the ancient Hebrews, meant a separation of the breath from the body. This "breath" was the "spirit" which would exist in Sheol. This was the Hebrew term for the underworld, the abode of the dead. They did not divide man into body and soul the way we do; the person was seen as a complete unit. The body/soul dichotomy was basic to later Greek thought, especially Platonism, and became prevalent in Christian thought.

Sheol was not thought of as a place of punishment for the wicked. Both good and bad went there. It was a gloomy, shadowy place, similar to the idea of Hades in Homer's *Odyssey*. It was a place of inactivity (Is 38:18) and existence there could scarcely be called "life."

The idea grew that God could deliver His friends from this place (cf. 1 S 2:6; Ps 49:16; 73:23–28). In later Jewish writings, around the second and third centuries before Christ, this was developed into the belief that there would be a resurrection of the dead. Dn 12:2, Is 53:11 and 2 M 14:46 illustrate this point.

Although the Hebrews believed in individual and collective rewards and punishments from God in this world (cf. Gn 12:17; Nb 16:27–30; Dt 28), they were late in coming to believe that this was the case in the afterlife. Their ideas on this gradually clarified (partly under the influence of Zoroastrian and Platonic ideas), and by the time of Jesus many Jews had well-developed ideas about rewards and punishments in the next world.

The Testimony of the New Testament

In his Letter to the Romans, Paul states that death is the consequence of sin and a punishment for it (Rm 5:12f). He also speaks of death as a prelude to the eternal reward (Ph 1:23) and to the general resurrection (1 Th 5:4–8). In Paul's vision, Christians have gone from death to life; they are raised to a new spiritual life with Christ.

The other New Testament writers also speak of death. They often treat it as a prelude to the general resurrection (Mt 24:42–44; Mk 13:33–37; Lk 21:34–36). They also consider the death of the just person (Mt 25:31–40; Lk 16:22). Death is seen as a one-time event. There is no reincarnation (Lk 16:26; Jn 9:4; 2 Cor 5:10; Heb 9:27).

They seldom speak of retribution taking place on earth. This idea is rejected by Jesus (Lk 9:51–56; Jn 9:2f). However, there is a definite retribution after death: happiness will be the lot of the just (Mt 5:12); a treasure is laid up in Heaven for them (Lk 12:33); they will enter into the joys of the Lord (Mt 25:21, 23). The unjust will be punished (Mt 8:12; 22:13). Paul's ideas are similar (1 Th 5:3; Ph 1:28; 2 Cor 5:1; 1 Tm 6:9).

The New Testament speaks of two judgments: the particular and the general. The particular judgment concerns each individual after death (Lk 16:19–31; 2 Cor 5:10; 2 Tm 4:6–8; Heb 10:31). The general judgment is seen as the great conclusion of all history. This is called different names: "the day" (Rm 13:12; 1 Th 5:4); "the last day" (Jn 6:39f); "the day of the Lord" (Ac 2:20; 1 Cor 5:5); "the day of Christ Jesus" (Ph 1:6); "the day of redemption" (Ep 4:30); and "the day of judgment" (Mt 10:15).

Precisely when the general judgment will take place is not clear. When asked about this, Jesus refused to say. "As to the exact day or hour, no one knows it, neither the angels in Heaven, nor even the Son, but only the Father" (Mk 14:32). "The exact time is not yours to know. The Father has reserved that to Himself" (Ac 1:7). There will be signs before it happens (Rm 11:25–26; 2 Th 2:1–12). The problem is how to interpret these biblical statements. The general judgment is presented in terms and images common in the religious thought of Jesus' day. Speculation is not of much use here. What is clear is that we must be vigilant and prepared (Mt 24:42–44; Mk 13:33–37; Lk 12:39f; 1 Th 5:1–6; 2 P 3:3–10).

The particular and general judgment are seen in connection with the resurrection of the body. The New Testament makes this point clear. The resurrection of the body is one of the basic beliefs of Christianity, deriving from the teachings of Jesus. It is stressed in the Synoptics: Mt 5:29f; 10:28; Mk 9:42–47; Lk 14:14. In John's Gospel, this resurrection will be effected by Christ (Jn 6:39f). Paul refers to it: 1 Cor 6:14; Ph 3:10f; 1 Th

4:13–17; 2 Tm 2:18. Acts (23:8; 26:6f) and Revelation (20:4–6, 11–15) also mention it.

The New Testament makes it clear that there is an afterlife. There will be a resurrection of the body. There will be a particular and general judgment. The just will be rewarded and the unjust will .be punished. The resurrection is a promise of the spiritual life already possessed by the risen Jesus and given to those who believe in Him.

The Official Teaching of the Church

The early Church writers reflect the biblical belief in the resurrection of the dead. And so, they passed on the apostolic tradition. Let us briefly examine some of these writings.

Justin Martyr (2nd century) in his *First Apology* mentions belief in the resurrection of the body. Athenagoras (2nd century) states, in his *Treatise on the Resurrection of the Dead*, that God will raise the dead body of every person to eternal life. Origen (3rd century) in his *Against Celsus* speaks of the last judgment and its rewards and punishments. Many others, such as Hippolytus and Tertullian, also refer to the resurrection. While some early Church Fathers erred on some particular points of the idea of the resurrection, their main ideas are correct. They linked the Christian's resurrection on the last day to Christ's Resurrection. Augustine (5th century), in *The City of God* and *On Perseverance*, spoke at length about the resurrection of the body and about rewards and punishments.

The Church Fathers of these first centuries set forth, in their writings, the doctrines which were handed down by the apostles. They laid the foundations for Christian theology. They led the Church in its encounter with non-Christian religions and philosophies of the ancient world.

The following are some Papal and Conciliar statements about the afterlife and the resurrection. For clarity, they have been divided by topic.

Death Using the Bible and Augustine, the Council of Trent (16th century) stated as an article of Faith that death is a punishment of sin. The Second Vatican Council (20th century) elaborated on the reality of death and its universal importance.

Judgment The last judgment is mentioned in the Apostles' Creed (date uncertain), the Nicene Creed (325), the Nicaeo-Constantinopolitan Creed (381), the Athanasian Creed (5th century), and by the Fourth Lateran Council (1215), the Second Council of Lyons (1274), the Constitution "Benedictus Deus" of Pope Benedict XII (1336), the Council of Florence (1439) and by the Second Vatican Council (1962–1965) in its *Pastoral Constitution on the Church in the Modern World*. The general judgment is an article of faith. The particular judgment follows from the dogma that each person will be judged for his or her own actions. The parable of Dives and Lazarus presupposes a particular judgment before the end of the world (Lk 16:19–31).

The Resurrection of the Dead The main creeds (Apostles', Nicaeo-Constantinopolitan, Athanasian) mention this, as do several General Councils (Fourth Lateran Council, Second Council of Lyons, Second Vatican Council).

The basic beliefs about death and resurrection, and judgment and retribution (Heaven, Hell, Purgatory) are dogmas of the Church and must be held by every Catholic. However, there are many open questions: when the judgment will take place, what the resurrected life will be like, what the sufferings of Purgatory and Hell consist of, etc.

Comment

Belief in the afterlife is firmly rooted in Jesus' teachings preserved in the Gospels. From the days of the apostles, these teachings were passed on to each new Christian generation. Through all her troubles, the Church professed that there is a Kingdom greater than any the present world has to offer. Through all adversity, she has clung to the hope that the just will be glorified forever, body and soul, and will experience the beatific vision of God. Unfortunately, some people lost sight of the whole picture, concentrating on lurid and imaginative aspects of punishment, and dwelling excessively on the images of fire and brimstone. The Second Vatican Council stressed God's loving forgiveness and the power of grace. In its pastoral concern, it stressed that grace is everywhere and works in all aspects of life. For the Christian, the Last Judgment brings all things to completion and is the ultimate grace. Then there will be perfect happiness, and eternal joy and love.

Special Questions

Is there a Purgatory and a Hell?
We have already said "yes" to this. Purgatory and Hell exist.

Purgatory is the gateway into Heaven, the final preparation for the wondrous vision of God. It is not a cosmic concentration camp. The Eastern and Western Churches agree on its existence, but they differ on particulars about it. For example, the Eastern Orthodox never accepted the idea of material fire there. Today, a more satisfying picture of the purgation process is emerging that may prove ultimately acceptable to Protestants as well as to Orthodox. The Church teaches that no one can enter Heaven burdened with the guilt and shame that remains even after sins are forgiven. Theologians speculate that as long as some type of restitution is not accomplished for our sins we refuse to forgive ourselves. We torture ourselves for hurting those we love even after they have sincerely forgiven us. This is the state of those in Purgatory. Their salvation is assured and Christ's love for them is clear. But this adds to their sense of shame, and for the first time they see the full extent of the damage of their sins. They refuse to look to the face of God out of the most profound embarrassment. The prayers of their loved ones on earth and of the

Church as a whole reassure them and urge them to look to the future, not the past, and to accept the pure gift of the vision of the Father that Christ offers them. These prayers are of immense importance to the person. Those praying agree that the person was imperfect and made mistakes, but they understand and urge him or her to accept that final place the Lord is giving them. A voice saying "Well done, My good and faithful servant, enter My Kingdom" is heard from the Lord Himself and through His entire Body in Heaven and on earth, and this voice draws the person into Heaven. We may say of this what Socrates says of his description of the afterlife and judgment in Plato's *Phaedo*: "No sensible man would think it proper to rely on things of this kind being just as I have described; but that, since the soul is clearly immortal, this or something like this at any rate is what happens in regard to our souls."

Hell, too, is a dogma of faith. Its existence is clear from the Bible and from the teachings of the Church. However, the New Testament images of fire, chains and weeping need not be taken literally. The essence of Hell is to be cut off from the God of love. It is a freely chosen eternity of aloneness, self-hatred and hatred of others. The Church has never defined that anyone is actually in Hell; she does say that Hell exists as a possibility for those who totally and deliberately reject God's love.

We do not have to worry about Hell if we remain firm in the love of God. We are dealing with a loving and merciful God, not a cruel tyrant.

What about cremation?

There was a time in the Catholic Church when cremation was forbidden. The reason for it was that the Masons and other anti-Catholic groups in Europe had their members cremated as a sign against the Resurrection. Those days have disappeared. Therefore, the Church allows cremation but still holds burial to be normative and can refuse Church funeral rites for those who choose cremation for anti-Christian motives. Several points should be made: 1) there is a funeral rite for cremation services; 2) the ashes do not have to be buried in the ground—they may be disposed of another way; 3) the feelings of the surviving relatives should be considered; 4) cremation destroys the possibility of leaving organ transplants (corneas, kidneys, etc.).

Discussion Questions

1. Explain the Jewish and the Greek concept of a human being.
2. What is Sheol?
3. What does the Second Book of Maccabees say about the Jewish notion of the resurrection of the dead?
4. From the Old Testament, show that the Jews believed in collective and individual retribution.
5. Why is the Book of Daniel important to the discussion on the resurrection of the dead?
6. Why is reincarnation not acceptable to Christianity?
7. Discuss the different terms for the General Judgment.
8. Our belief in the resurrection of the dead comes from Jesus' teachings. Discuss the New Testament evidence.
9. What did the early Church Fathers say about the resurrection of the dead?
10. What is the Church's official position on the Judgment?
11. What must a Catholic absolutely believe about the resurrection of the dead?
12. What must a Catholic believe concerning Purgatory and Hell? What is open to speculation?

EPILOGUE: A DOGMATIC REFLECTION

We have examined the basic beliefs of the Roman Catholic Church expressed in the ancient Apostles' Creed.

Christians accept and commit themselves to these beliefs which are rooted in the revelation of God. This revelation was not given all at once. For Christians, Jesus is the ultimate revelation of God. "In times past, God spoke in fragmentary and varied ways to our Fathers through the prophets; in this, the final age, He has spoken to us through His Son" (Heb 1:1–2).

The word "dogma" refers either to a particular belief (i.e., the Trinity) or to a whole system of beliefs (i.e., Christian beliefs as distinct from Moslem beliefs). That is why we have said that the Creed contains the basic beliefs (dogmas) of the Roman Catholic Church. Dogmas must be accepted by everyone who wishes to be considered Catholic.

The official Church (the Magisterium) functions to protect and hand on these basic beliefs for future Christian generations. The Magisterium (an Ecumenical Council whose head is always the Pope, or the Pope speaking as head of the universal Church but apart from a Council) issues a solemn decree clarifying its position on a particular dogma in question. For example, Pope Pius XII defined the Assumption of the Blessed Virgin Mary as a dogma of the Church. However, he did not act arbitrarily in this matter. He only acted after extensive consultation with the laity and the bishops of the world concerning their opinion on this issue. It is interesting to note that this Marian doctrine had long been accepted by the majority of the Church membership. The Pope made official the doctrine unofficially believed.

Dogmatic discussions, explorations and challenges seek further insights.

Dogmas, however, are formed through human expressions of belief. Like any human expression, they are subject to the limitations of language, style and cultural expression. At times it becomes necessary for the Magisterium to reformulate a dogmatic statement. Dogmas are not static, but dynamic. They are living ideas with deeper implications. In the past the Church Fathers, the General Councils and the Popes preserved and reformulated the dogmas for their age. Today, the same challenge remains.

The German theologian, Michael Schmaus, summarized it very well: "Since the Church has to proclaim the message of salvation until the end of time, and the absolute future until its arrival, she will never cease to wrestle intellectually with the challenge presented by the world; and so likewise, the Church will never cease to develop dogma. In this respect also, the Church must remain open to whatever the future may bring." (*Dogma*, p. 253)

INDEX